T0077359

OUT OF THE DARKNESS

LILLY FAITH

BALBOA.
PRESS
A DIVISION OF HAY HOUSE

Balboa Press books may be ordered through booksellers or by contacting:

Balboa Press
A Division of Hay House
1663 Liberty Drive
Bloomington, IN 47403
www.balboapress.com.au
1 (877) 407-4847

Printed in the United States of America.

ISBN: 978-1-4525-1340-9 (sc)
ISBN: 978-1-4525-1339-3 (e)

Balboa Press rev. date: 3/27/2014

Contents

About Words

Was this it? Was this really all that life had to offer me? Nothing but pain anguish and loneliness a sensation that was beyond numb, struggling to wake every morning just to survive another day. Forever wishing that it was just a bad dream that I would wake from yet so deeply knowing that I had died inside and all that was left was killing off my body taking all presence away, stopping the rhythm my heartbeat made and cutting off all breathe. For if I wasn't there then what reason was there for my body to be and if for some chance that there was a reason I just could not see it.

I had attempted to take my life on a few occasions over the years but this was different I wasn't taking my life. How could I be when there was no sign of life left inside absolutely nothing, I could not feel, I could not think I had reached the end of life itself unable to feel not even the pain, anguish, hurt or anger that had kept me here all of these years was present any longer this must have been how my life was meant to end. Not my children's love could take this burden from me nor the drugs and alcohol I put into my body just to try to feel to know what it was like to be anything other, then what I was.

I was trapped in this space of nothingness screaming to just end it all, how could I possibly stay here any longer and keep my body alive when I was truly beyond sadness and any glimmer of hope or return. I would hear words coming from my mouth but were they mine? Me? Who was I? Did I even know who I had ever been and who were these people they didn't love me why were they making me or even Wanting me to stay in this life I had given up on surviving fighting the so called good fight.

GOD what kind of divine, mighty, loving being would have inflicted such a life upon me pure survival itself I had lost all determination and motivation to keep going there was no purpose for my life. Unable to see anything other than a means to an end, I was in complete consuming darkness sent here for the brutal pleasure of others into a life of hell having everyone I had ever tried to love, leave me abandoned and walking along my path alone there was no light had I ever felt what love was in my life.

All of these questions stuck in my mind overtaking everything I could not comprehend anything other than the need to die to be taken away from all of this, hearing what my children were saying to me but not understanding their needs, how could I love my children when I couldn't understand what it meant to love? They were the sole reason I woke every morning I bought them into this horrible existence of mine they were MY cross to bare.

As I sat there what used to be haunting memories were now nothing I had no comprehension of what was real and what was not, all I knew was that the lights were on but I had been missing for years sending my carbon copy in until now it was time, time to end it all to finally have the strength to succeed. It was in the next moment that everything changed and my journey began.

CHAPTER 1

Innocence Lost

My story of anguish started the day I was born into this existence the youngest memory I have was sitting on the concrete path outside of our home with my two older brothers, Wayne and Shaun excited with our bags packed waiting for our dad to come and get us but sadly he did not come it was not the first time this happened waiting for him to come and take me away and love me.

The last childhood memory I had of the man left me confused and not understanding why he did not come back and where had he gone? On this night I woke to a very big noise my dad had put his hand through our front door and there were blue and red lights outside, he tried to take me with him and I couldn't understand why mum wouldn't let my dad back to live with us and why she was so sad. I grew up with my mum and her partner my stepdad who I had to call dad the one who would drastically beat me all through my childhood years and constantly put me down, calling me horrible names and a pathetic excuse for a person. I'm not exactly sure of when my mum and my stepdad met what I do remember is seeing my mum smiling and acting funny when he was at our home if he was a loving person then I never got to experience it.

There is no loving memories that I hold with him as he was to be named "the monster" who made my brothers wet their beds in fear when they were teenage boys, the monster that inflicted brutal punishment abuse and control even as I grew into an adult. It is true that emotional scars stay a lot longer than physical not only can it cut so deep into your being but stay with you for a life time or more. The first brutal attack happened when I was in year 1 at school, to this day I'm not sure what I had done wrong or hadn't done maybe I was just being a happy child more than likely it was because I had not done a job that had been given to me.

I recall being taken into my mums bedroom where a red piece of cloth was shoved into my mouth like a bandanna and I was made to lay across the bed as the jug cord lashed my backside sting after sting, it felt like forever my backside red roar finding it difficult to breath and cry through the cloth in my mouth. Weeks later some ladies came to my school to ask me about what had happened how did they know? I was going to be in so much trouble and I was so scared that he would find out!

I told the ladies that nothing happened and that's the way it had to be as much as I wanted to cry and tell them everything I just couldn't! A few weeks later, I ran away from home. I was scared and petrified who would help us who could I tell to take this monster away? My memory still so clear of the day before some-one had taken a cheese stick from the fridge and eaten it!

This so called stealing happened a lot growing up and I cannot blame any of them if I had, had the guts I would have done it also, we were very hungry so if they had to take food then of course they could not and would not own up to it. As we grew older one of us would eventually take the blame anything to make the blows stop, because we all knew he took great delight in hitting into us taunting and torturing us, but this brutal day was one of the most horrific experiences that I had ever endured in my short life. My brothers were either not silly enough or brave enough to own up to who took the cheese stick from the fridge and the monster was getting nowhere, after what seemed like a long time beating into my brothers and I and yelling the monster took one of his treasured swords out.

I started to shake my brothers and I were all crying it was always me, I was always first to be picked to endure the brunt of it along with my older brother Shaun, and the much loved mother that I held so dear to my heart where was she? Always hiding somewhere allowing it to all happen?

The monster grabbed my arm and forced it onto a table I was so petrified and my little body could not stop shaking, I completely lost all sensations of my body and could feel a hot sensation running down my legs I had wet myself I heard the monster saying that they cut thieves hands off who steal as he pressed the blade into the tops of my knuckles, it must have been my screams of terror that bought my mum out of hiding because she yelled something and he let me go I ran, I ran so fast out of the front door I did not know where I was to go I had no-one that I could run to for help.

Why wouldn't someone help me? Who would listen to me my little head was starting to hurt as I stood dead still crying not able to move until my mum came out and told me to get back inside. She took me into her room I could hear my brothers crying I had wet myself and I was in a state of absolute terror where was my mums hugs.

Was she not supposed to tell me she loved me and its okay faith I'll never let anyone hurt you I did not hear that instead my mum asked me if it was me who took the cheese stick. It was at this time in my life that I had my first out of body experience my body was in shock and my little mind could not take what was happening so I left, I left my body and that horrible place at 7 yrs old and began a life of lost memories that I would not remember until I was well into my adult years I spent most of my life gone my body present but no-one inside.

Constantly seeing what was happening my body being beaten and the beautiful person I may have been inside was no longer alive, realising that no-one loved me no-one cared if I could only disappear. Each year that went by the taunts and put downs became more and more intense along with the physical abuse was the hatred I would see in the monsters eyes towards us more so my brother Shaun and I, videos of emotional scarring, being made to feel and believe that I was worth nothing. Concerts or performances at school knowing that my mum wouldn't be there watching me with love and pride the way mothers should, the only time I do recall was at a school carnival and I had just run the fastest and won a first ribbon I loved it I loved the feeling of running. I was running from myself, from my life as I got to the finish line I saw my mum under a tree smiling I ran over happy and excited to see her there the monster was beside her but I did not care my mum saw me she really saw me.

A little while after that day mum told us that they were having a new baby how exciting this was and when we found out we were having a baby sister my whole world changed, the day came that my beautiful sister Sarah was born, and that was the first time I witnessed the monster as a loving person he would fuss over her and love her the way I had never witnessed anyone in my life love another. To me it felt like he tried to keep me away from mum and sarah as much as possible, the emotional and physical abuse escalated when his daughter came into the world, the more love and pride and all the feelings that a parent is supposed to feel for their child the more hate and disgust we took on, I can't say that my mum was aware of what was happening because she spent a lot of her life in a daze

I can be sure that I did not know what love or even true happiness was, I would hide myself in my own fanciful world with my beautiful little sister when I could but most of the time we had to sit back and witness just how much we really were despised by the way they would love her. It wasn't always that way, when we would go camping it was exciting because my mum was happy she would have this sort of unspeakable light inside of her when I did see that side I cherished it, a spark of hope would be ignited, I admired and loved her while my little heart ached desperately for her to love me and to hold me.

My favourite time was when she would let me brush her beautiful long hair I was so close to her just wanting to put my arms around her and cuddle her but I couldn't the monster wouldn't allow it! He took her away from me. I was only 2 when he stole my mum from me never to get to have her hold me and tell me she loved me, seeing other kids with loving parents always hoping mum would take us away he didn't love us and we could love and look after our mum she didn't need him. How could this be my life, the thought of being able to just hug my mum, and tell her I loved her striking a deep fear within me.

Anything that was to do with love was to be feared. When my new baby sister stephanie came along 2 years later yet again I fell in love with her just as I did with sarah I would sit on my mums bed watching her beautiful little eyes staring up at me smiling and making loving noises she was amazing I was older now so I got to hold her and sing to her.

I never let anyone see that side of me how could I it was wrong and I would probably go through some sort of reprimand for it, it was as though my little sister and I had our own little secret she was very special to me. When Stephanie was only a few months old mum and the monster told us that there was a house for us to look at because the home we were in was too small for all of us it was all so very exciting and everyone seemed to be happy and in good spirits we stopped outside of a big highset home the words that came from my mum were wonderful she was in tears and shock "this can't be it" but it was.

The next few days went by amazingly my mum was happily packing if I was yelled at or put down I did not care because my mum was so happy and it was a new life for us. I spent the days leading up to the move holding and singing to my beautiful sister Stephanie and watching Sarah, running around playing then the day came that we made the move into our beautiful new home.

I'm not sure why but for some strange unknown reason it was in my head that because my mum was different and happy that she would learn to love me and wouldn't allow anything horrible or anyone to hurt us again that we would have no more brutal punishments or put downs that I had endured for many years. I didn't know it then but I was horribly wrong in such a significant way, for it was in this house that I lost what was my childhood, my innocence and descended into a life of pure loneliness, hatred and darkness.

Each day that went by I watched my beloved mother lose herself there was only sadness. I can't say how I knew this I just felt it a pure sadness, I tried to stay close to her, and would feel safe which would completely confuse me as all my heart did was ache for my mum ache for some sort of love for some-one to tell me they loved me and I wasn't a mistake or a burden to them that I wasn't worthless.

Not understanding how they could love my two sisters and not me what was so wrong with me? Had I made them hate me? What could I do to make them love me? The only relief that I had from all of the turmoil was when I would escape into my room and transport into another life when I opened a book, I could not put them down I had to keep reading because the moment I did when the story stopped I was me again the ugly, horrible person that everyone hated.

Starting a new school and making friends I got to be a kid again I was able to have sleep overs at my best friend Beccy's, although her life was completely different to mine, I could not confide in her about what was happening. I enjoyed going to her home I would have to drink soy milk and take vitamins every morning and listen to her dad read out of the bible or preach about GOD, But I did not mind because no-one was hurting me and she was my first real friend but mum could not stand her so it wasn't long before I was not allowed to be her friend anymore I was removed, from the school and sent to another and lost contact with her.

Any friends I was alienated from, my life gradually became a blur of beatings and belittling. One of the silliest things that I would constantly do was not eat my lunch at school and would bring it home, one afternoon I was standing at the top of the stairs being yelled at in trouble for not eating my lunch. I could never understand why it was such a horrible, wrong thing, to not be hungry and enjoy my time at school, or just sit under a tree and read my book and actually play with my friends.

This particular afternoon I thought that I was going to be thrown down the stairs but it was much worse. He grabbed me and put his hands around my throat, I thought that was it, he was going to kill me and I didn't care. The chaotic thoughts going through my head he would be arrested and go to jail and my mum would finally be free! My brothers would never have to hurt again and I would be in a better place far from, where I was able to watch over my family forever. But nothing happened and as I opened my eyes his horrible scary face was right near mine, eyes so red with hate and rage. Why didn't he do it? Why didn't he just end it and again my mum where was she where was my mum when he did this and all the other brutal punishments he would inflict? Could she hear the yelling?

The cries and screaming just because I was breathing and not care, not care that all I wanted was for this horrible evil monster to be gone, gone from us. From the ones I loved even if I could not have her love, he could kill me and would have accomplished the Inevitable. he would never get to hurt one of them again, or make my mum live a life of sadness. She could be free and happy. Becuase It was only one day a year that was the happiest day of my life and that was christmas.

Mum would exceed all of my expectations for that time of the year we would have a big beautiful tree and decorations were put up all over the house. That day we would receieve such awesome presents the day spent laughing, playing and eating. Oh how we would eat! It was always mum up first when we would walk down the stairs and open the door. She would be sitting there with a big smile on her face and you just knew that my real mum, was in there, I would go to bed that night so happy. Full of yummy food and just even for a moment before I went off to sleep feel happy for being alive.

Every day of our lives in that home we had the same routine we were his soldiers and he the major, the boss when we were told to do something it was efficient and done quickly or we would be punished. Chased around the house with a cane stick being whipped for not going fast enough everything absolutely everything had to be done his way and that was it! Why wouldn't he just leave? why did he stay and hurt us take our childhood away? living in fear cringing about what was going to happen?

Mum started spending time in her room in her bed leaving us with him, constant let downs being told that we were going to be going somewhere on the weekend "anywhere was better than that house" forever waiting for it to happen sitting upstairs, looking out of the window tears running down my face, knowing my hopes were fading away oh how I prayed and dreamed for a new life.

Having to sit in the hallway eating cold baked beans and bread while the monster cooked yummy food, that we could smell our tummy's rumbling being made to witness my two sisters mum and the monster eating take away or better food then what we had. They would go out and always bring back a special little treat for the girls. I watched my mum fade away and start putting on a large amount of weight and would not want to do anything unless it was staying home and cleaning, or she thoroughly enjoyed going to the dump shop and bringing home things, that is where most of our stuff came from the clothes we would wear were never new the only clothes my mum ever bought me from a shop were 2 very beautiful cheese cloth dresses that would be taken away from me and used as a weapon of manipulation against me.

When we finally met our next door neighbour his name was Duncan I thought he was such a lovely man and he started coming over and becoming friends with mum and the monster and eventually I still do not remember how but my sisters and I would start going over to his house for movies. He would take me to the markets, to his parents' house and other outings. He was like the dad I longed for always, giving me cuddles, making us yummy food to eat and spoil us rotten with Ice-cream and lollies, I wished that he was my dad; he would play around with my brothers and spend a lot of time with us. My favourite past time was when we were in his room looking at all of his amazing coins from all over the world, listening to his stories and dreaming about all of the places he would secretly tell me that he was going to take me to, he knew about the monster.

Sarah would always come over with me and play with his little dog Suzy except for the first day that it was just me, I had just watched gummi bears and Duncan called me into his room he put me on his lap and told me that it was okay. He knew that no-one loved me and he would keep me safe and he gave me a big hug.

My heart beat so fast knowing that I would never have a bruise that was blamed on my clumsiness that I would never have a soar, weak body again. He laid me on the bed and told me to have a sleep, I cuddled up to the pillows in the warm comfy bed.

My little heart hurt knowing that I would have to leave my mum when he took me away and I drifted off to sleep. I'm not sure how long I may have slept for but it was when I awoke I endured the first reoccuring theme of my life. Duncan was touching me in a way I had never experienced,(he was performing oral sex on me) what was he doing? he told me was that it was our secret that no-one could ever know.

My little mind was trying to understand as a memory came of walking into my mums room the monster was doing the same thing and my mum was making strange noises. I closed my eyes and dreamed of a life with my new dad, it was a strange feeling. I had never had that before no-one, had ever done that to me he got up and smiled at me and asked if I wanted a sandwich? I said yes but I wanted to go home and have a bath Duncan said that I could have a shower and to just remember it was our little secret that he loved me and was going to take me away.

He was waiting to find someone to buy his home that was just the beginning, of what became a regular event. Every time, I was in his house, I would be made to take my undies off as he would do that time and time again. Duncan began to get very angry a lot and that scared me he told me that no matter what that I wasn't to tell anyone, our little secret because if I did he could not take me away. There were times that he would make me touch him and he touch me. Why was he doing this? Any chance that he was given, I was confused and angry because if I asked my mum and told her I would be breaking the secret that was going to take me away from that horrible place.

I could not understand and I began to feel hate towards him, even more when he started seeing a lady called Debbie, who I heard mum saying was over 20 years younger than him. There was one night that my mum called me into her room and asked if Duncan had ever touched me. Oh how I wished that I could tell mum, but I couldn't. They would hate me even more than what they already did! What was I to say to mum it was a secret I promised that I would never say anything, even when my anger grew that Duncan stopped talking to me and letting us go over there because he married Debbie and they had a baby. I would hear mum and the monster talking about them all of the time.

How could he have hurt me and promised me that I was safe that he would be my dad, why? What did I ever do to anyone why did people hate me and not want me was I really that bad of a person? Any one that my mum and the monster befriended it wasn't for long because it would seem that the other people would do something wrong or they did or had something better than us. I spent many years listening to the monster proclaiming he was GOD that he knew everything and was never wrong everyone else was! I tried to look after my brothers as much as I could, not once did I ever fight with them never did my beautiful brothers hurt me. I loved throwing the football around with them and playing in the cubby house and I loved absolutely loved our animals.

We had an old English sheepdog tiny and a beautiful big Alaskan Malamute who was called tom. When I wasn't cleaning up and going to the dump shop to find a special new possession or maybe a new piece of clothing, I was reading. The constant belittling and abuse just became an everyday occurrence some days worse than others. It depended on what I had or hadn't done or how much anger or hatred that the monster had to show for on the day, then came a day that would stain, tarnish and imprint my heart for long years.

I met Uncle Frank he was a handsome funny, loving man that came to live with us I remember he was a painter and slept on the fold out couch in our downstairs lounge room it was wonderful having him around, because the worst we would endure would be getting spoken to like we were nothing, and the quiet threats it did not matter because everyone seemed so happy the whole house hold changed my mum was out of her room and always laughing I could vaguely remember meeting him and his baby daughter years before and I learnt, that he was my little sister Sarah's god father and my mums best friend of many years before I was born. He would laugh and play even the monster seemed different while he was there.

Wow I would go to bed at night for a week trying to work out in my head how having this man in our home had changed everything, especially the way my mum would light up when he was around. On the 8th night "I remember, because I counted the days to see how long it would last"

I was asleep in my bed and felt my blanket being pulled down away from me and then I was being picked up and carried down the hallway then down the stairs, it was uncle Frank he was talking a little funny and smelt like smokes and the beer he would drink all I kept thinking in my mind was what is happening?

I was scared and confused this wasn't Uncle Frank. He would not make me scared and hurt me. It was what happened next that not only violated my body but stole my soul. My clothes were taken off and, just like Duncan had done only a year or so before he performed oral sex on me but it wasn't like before it hurt, and my body jolted then I felt something I tried to move my body but I couldn't it wouldn't move. It hurt, for a moment I thought it was over, it had stopped. And I had survived but how wrong I was. It wasn't over, he pulled his pants off and brutally raped me, what came next was the most excruciating pain from within me.

I was screaming inside where was my mum if only she could hear me, why what had I ever done why was this happening? My head began to hurt so badly and the pain was unbearable and then it stopped, but I was no longer in my body. I was above it. watching everything that was happening, tears running down my pale white face. My body was being so brutally ravished and then something even more horrifying happened. I was made to perform oral sex on him.

I was back in my body and I could hardly breathe! I wanted to throw up and I wanted to die. I just wanted it to stop, He helped me put my pyjamas back on and told me if I ever told mum she would not believe me or care.

He carried me back upstairs and put me into bed as I lay in bed my eyes wide open my body so sore, and my heart thumping hard in my chest.

I cried for my mum, I cried and ached, for my mum. Why did she not love me, how could she let this happen? I didn't even know what just happened to me nor did I realise that it would happen for months nearly every night time after, time after, time. Constantly, he would violate my body completely.There was not a spot that was not touched, hurt or violated what used to be sacred was no longer safe and it only became harder and faster he would tell me One night that I was getting good at this now and to try to move my hips a bit that he wanted me He loved me.

Every morning I woke violently sick, my body sore, my heart heavy, and my head feeling like it wanted to explode. Left feeling nothing but weak I did not want to wake up. Where was my mum? Did she know what was happening? How could I be here when I was so unloved, a burden a thorn in everyone's side, a pathetic excuse for a human being?

Told I would never amount to anything I was stupid a hypochondriac, lazy a waste of space, abused for being sick and when I wasn't enduring my body being violated every night. I was sick and being so badly beaten! I begged and prayed for it to stop. That my mum would make it stop, or that he would hurt me so badly that it took my life. I knew that I wouldn't be able to survive another night and then it finally came the day that my body was left alone, Uncle Frank had found a girlfriend and was moving out.

It wasn't until after he left and it had completely stopped and I knew in my head that it would never happen again, that I descended into pure hatred for life for myself I started leaving my body often because I would blank I was regularly getting called stupid, ditzy, deaf earth to Faith are you there? It got me into trouble, because I was accused of not listening. I did not want to go to school anymore! I was used to staying home and cleaning anything, to not be near people. I hated everyone and tried to stay close to my mum, so close because she rarely left her room anymore.

I just wanted and needed for her to love me, to hold me, anything so I could pour my heart out and tell her everything. But like my whole life that did not happen. I was in pure darkness and I wanted to take my life! I wanted it to all go away, the pain, I felt I could not bare anymore.

CHAPTER 2

All Hope diminished

The day that it became apparent to me that I could do it, I could take my life. I was in my mum's bathroom downstairs because I was being made to clean it. I opened the cupboard on the wall to put something in I saw the highly toxic flea wash that we used on the dogs, just sitting there. I saw my hand reach out and pick it up. Could it really be this easy? All I had to do was swallow it and I could die! I could end it all! I didn't want to be here anymore, I wanted a break from my life. I didn't want this pain within myself anymore!

Yes, yes I could do it! I opened the tin, it smelt awful a smell I hated and knew so well from washing the dogs. My stomach twisted and clenched, I kept saying in my head it's the only way Faith, it's the only way. Even if just for a little break, just a little break from the pain just to sleep and not wake up for a while. I had to get away; I had to get away from myself. I put it to my lips and took a huge gulp…

Yuk it burnt my throat and hurt and when it reached my stomach. I instantly felt sick I put the lid back on and stayed in the bathroom, for what seemed like a long time. I was starting to feel very sick, I saw my reflection in the mirror, my face a pale white and sweat pouring from me everywhere what had I done?

I would never get to see my mum again how could she ever learn to love me if I was dead? My heart was hurting and beating rapidly fast in my chest and my body shaking, I had to tell mum the truth I had to tell her before it was too late! As I walked out to the lounge room to let it all out, I froze I couldn't instead I heard myself saying that I had accidently swallowed the poison. All I remember after that was waking in the hospital in intensive care, with sticky things that were monitoring my heart and tubes coming from me. I was so sick and trembling cold I could not stop shaking and it was now night time my mum was next to me she looked sad and she spoke to me in such a soft tone.

I ached so much for my mum to cuddle me, to hold me to tell me that she loved me and life was going to be a lot better now that I was still here. But just like the story of what had become my life, it did not come not even when I drank poison. What was wrong with me? I wondered why did GOD not take me why was I still here? Why did I even bother telling anyone when I could have just quietly died in the bathroom and no-one would have known until it was too late?

I stayed in the hospital for days and eventually started feeling better, I had people come and talk to me and ask if I had tried to take my life because no-one could understand how it had all happened. I couldn't tell anyone it was my secret so I just kept saying that it was an accident, that I would never do that! I loved my mum coming and visiting me and I knew it was my real mum, the beautiful person who I struggeled to understand.

I was eventually able to go home and for two or more whole days I was left alone and things did seem to get better for me. I loved going to school, I had again changed schools and met a wonderful great new best friend. Her name was teneil her family were great and our parents became friends. I was in year 7 and mum would let me go over to their home to have sleep overs and even better was when they moved just around the corner from me. Life for me was actually great. I loved school so much but the best thing was that the monster now had a job and he worked at night. I enjoyed being at home with my mum!

The real mum was with me again, because she was different and I could be so close to her so many happy nights I was living a dream. She did not tell me she loved me and the only body contact that I would get was when I would kiss her on the forehead goodnight, but that was enough for me, because I knew that life was great and as much as I would sometimes try to remember, I just could not it was as though to me the past had never happened, for some reason my mind would not allow me to remember anything.

The monster became less brutal because we would not see him and that suited all of us, My mum spent a lot less time in her room, she was smiling a lot more and life could not be better for me. I should have guessed it but nothing stayed happy for me and all of it changed drastically.

At school everyone was laughing and giggling about the family planning lesson that we were to have, when the time came we walked into the classroom the tables were all against the walls and everyone was sitting on the floor. Teneil and I were up the back talking about the sleep over that we were going to have on the weekend. When the lesson started there was a lady up the front of the class talking to us about men, women and what sex was and what was right and wrong and not consensual sex. All I can recall was a sudden pain in my head and then all of the awful memories of what Uncle Frank had done to me came rushing back. What was happening?

It all came back to me everything! He molested me that's what it was called! It had a name! I closed my eyes and when I opened them, I was underneath one of the tables on the side of the room. I was shaking and my head hurt badly, my heart was racing! I could not think and I was being violated over and over again in my mind. Everything all of the tastes and smells came back to me the sick feeling I felt in my stomach.

I must have blanked again and somehow told Teneil and her mum, otherwise I didn't know how they became aware all, I knew was that, on that night, I had to tell my mum before Teneil's mum did, I had to face what I had done.

I was sitting beside my mum later that night on the floor, my heart still beating rapidly because I had asked her that afternoon if I could talk to her after the monster went to work and now I was here. It was time; I could not hold it in anymore. I had to tell mum. My palms were sweaty. What was I supposed to say? My head full of thoughts and words it just all came out. I heard myself blurting it all out. Everything.

I was not on the floor next to mum anymore, I was above watching everything that was happening again I heard every word until I was back in my body left confused not understanding I had just told my mum about the most horrible thing I had ever experienced. The most sickening feeling and horrible tastes in my mouth. The smells taking over my body and nothing! she did not hold me or tell me that it was going to be ok or that it was not my fault it had happened. Anything to make me feel better and know that I did not deserve this.

Staring into the space, not able to hear anything I didn't want to hear I wished I was back in the bathroom and that I had made the choice to let the poison kill me until, some of the questions that my mum asked me brought me back. I went upstairs to bed, what was going to happen now? It seemed that she did not believe me. Was it just all a bad dream or a scary story that I had made up in my mind? No it wasn't, it was my fault that's what it was.

I wasn't able to make anyone love me. It was my fault! I deserved it to happen to me! What came next was being accused of lying by the monster... was I really sure that it was real that is wasn't just my imagination? I knew it wasn't, the memory so clear in my body the tastes in my mouth. It really did happen. My childlike innocence had been stolen. I had been raped. Not only my body my soul Why did I have to tell the police? Then everyone would have to know my shame and that it was my entire fault.

If only I hadn't of tried to love and be loved so much it was all my whole fault! What else could I expect from being so hated? I made it happen, why else would it have happened? Walking into the police station I was led into a dark room, my mum could not be with me. What was going to happen? Why was I even here, if it was me who made this happen then why did the police have to be told? Not only that, why did I have to live through it again what were the police going to do for me? It had happened already.

The officer, a kind lady, asked me all sorts of questions, I found myself stumbling on my words. I knew so well what had happened I had relived it since the day at school but I couldn't bring myself to say the words. A long time I spent in that room ashamed of what I had allowed to happen to me and then all of a sudden it was over. I was told that I could go. The officer tried to tell me that it was not my fault yet my own mother did not say a thing to me.

I knew it was because; she could not even look me in the eyes nor say a thing to me. Why did she not talk to me about anything of what the police did? Never a word to me! I knew I had disgraced her with all of the things, I allowed her friend and my uncle to do to me and I knew I deserved to be hated. Did they not realise that I already knew that? Next was a visit to the hospital. As I lay on the hospital bed while I had a swab, being taken I could not believe what was happening. Why now? What good would this do now it had already happened? What did they expect to find?

I had been hurt so badly, but it was years ago, I had suffered the pain already. What was this stupid thing going to do now? What more did I have to go through? What more would I have to suffer? I didn't know that they wanted me to go to court to tell them what had happened because Uncle Frank had to go to jail for what he did. I knew I had been the blame for what happened but he did hurt me. I never even for a second thought it was his fault.

I must have done something to make him hurt me in that way. I could not bring myself to say the word that they called it! But I was forced too. I was told I HAD to! What was I to expect every time I tried to think about the day that was coming? I would start to feel sick, everyone would learn my shame they would hear all of the things I let Uncle Frank do to me. I did not have to think too much about it because the day came before I had a chance to calm down and I found myself in a little room in the court house.

I had been told that Uncle Frank had to be in the same room but there would be a white board in front of him while they asked me some questions, from the night at the police station if I was scared? Of course I was scared! I didn't want to do any of this! I just wanted to jump into one of my books and escape into another life, another story or just fade into the pages. But this was my life! This was my story! I was here because I was so hated and I trusted someone to love me but instead I made them hurt me. I was exactly what the monster had said all of my life I worthless.

Sitting in the little room alone without my mum and Teneil because they had to speak in court as well. I was sitting with an old lady who was there to support me and make me feel comfortable, but this was the day that I had to face what I allowed happen to me. My heart was racing and hurting, my chest and my head full of thoughts I could not stop it. full of fear the door then opened and I was politely told it was time.

I was lead to the courtroom and told to sit at a little section with a chair. A man came over to me and told me to put my hand on the bible and I had to repeat after him. Why the bible GOD hated me and I hated him. Why did I have to swear on the bible when this so called GOD did not ever take me away or save me? I looked over at the whiteboard and it was not fear I was feeling anymore. A subtle rush came from within me. I felt so angry! Angry that I was sitting there and being asked stupid questions If no-one believed me. I had to sit there while the horrible nasty man was trying to call me a liar and asking me about what pyjamas I had worn back when it happened.

What kind of people would care about what pjs I had worn and if I still had them? I was beyond angry something inside of me was simmering. I could physically feel it! Who the hell were these people and what right did they have to be making me feel that way? I knew that no-one loved me and everyone I loved hurt me, whether I allowed it or not. Everything I said the horrible man tried to turn it back on me like I was lying that was nothing new to me. Being called a liar all of my life.

Maybe he had been talking to the monster? As I thought of the monster I looked over through the glass and there he was sitting watching. I could see tears what kind of right did he have to sit there Now when he didn't believe me When I had sworn to him that I wasn't lying! How could I have been, when my body would not allow me to forget? I didn't have to do this if they all believed that I was lying and just making this horror story up.

Then why couldn't they just leave me alone and let me go? It felt like I was stuck in that little spot for hours my head started hurting again and then there I was, above the courtroom watching myself answering questions with blank eyes. Not being able to remember everything and listening to what I had put into my statement.

I watched myself becoming more and more confused because the man was talking so fast and I was not able to keep up. Then the judge spoke and it was time to go. When I left that room that day I left a different person deep inside, I knew that I was never going to let anyone hurt me. From within I knew that somewhere a big piece of me died that day and what replaced it was pure hatred and anger! I would never allow myself to love anyone again I would never allow anyone near me! They could have my body but like hell were they ever getting my heart! I put a huge brick wall up that day and behind that brick wall I had entwined myself in a protective barrier so no-one would ever get close to me again!

CHAPTER 3

No Return

I would lay in bed at night pretending that I was someone different I just did not care. I was consumed with hate and anger. But there was a part of me that dare not close my eyes. That dare not dream, because soon my dreams became nightmares and I would wake soaked in sweat, shaking with fear. I'm not sure what I feared but it was there paralysed by it! What was next for me, could I bare it? I was just waiting to see what would come for me as much as I dreaded it, something inside of me was daring for the next big thing, so I could hate even more. So I could feel more pain, because that's what I survived on. That was all I knew.

If I had to suffer and feel pain for the rest of my life, anything to not give my heart that's what I would do. My mum called me into her room one morning and asked me to shut the door. This was it this was the next thing I could feel it. She looked at me with such caring eyes and said to me that she had tried to help me and just couldn't anymore. I needed help before I ended up in a bad place. What did she mean? I was living in a bad place; my life was the bad place. Was there something far worse than what I had already lived through? If there was bring it on! Why did she care? She hadn't cared when I needed her.

She hadn't held me or loved me when I needed it. Mum asked me to go with her and see someone I could talk to. Just maybe believe that she could help me and make me feel better. She told me that I had to see a therapist because everything had become a letter. I could not look at people and I would get angry and do stupid things, anything to feel the pain.

I chose to see the therapist for my mum I did want to get better, but something always held me back. I would completely block everything out with music. My beautiful therapist never pushed me. The first day I saw her I could not move she was a beautiful kind lady who was so soft. It took a few sessions for me to even speak to her. There were times that I would open up and try to explain what I was feeling. But then I would be consumed with fear. No I couldn't. I could not let anyone in I promised myself that I was to keep me safe. Safe in robot mode.

No way could I ever let anyone in I was ashamed of what I held inside, what hope did anyone have to understand me, when I couldn't even do that myself. It was safe for me to not open up to anyone and that's the way it had to be! Mum would never come in with me she would sit outside and when I walked out she would give me a beautiful smile. there was an unspoken understanding.

One session it came out that I was not sleeping so she made me my own special tapes and after some time of listening to them quietly in my room I eventually drift off to sleep. Not always but if I got some sleep during the night then it was progress for me. If I dared listen to music in my room the monster would always come thumping up the stairs to take the one thing away from me that could take the harshness of the pain away. Music. but I did not let anyone know my weakness. He knew because anything I did, that may have taken the force of darkness out of me or away even for a short time, he would take away from me. I came to believe that he was there to make me suffer, to make me live with this horrible darkness within me.

I did not have too many sessions with my therapist. The day came that I was asked to draw a picture of what was happening Inside of me after sitting for a while, staring with a blank look at the piece of paper and coloured pencils I found myself picking up the black pencil and what I drew was exactly what was happening. I was in a deep black tunnel and there was no light but the tiny little spec so far away from me, I could not reach it. In that moment I realised that there was no return. If I could not reach the light then how was anyone else going to help do it? I was a dark hating person, black became my favourite colour. I hated everything. My only friend who tried to be there for me as much as possible soon left to go back to Western Australia where she came from, it didn't matter to me.

Everyone, who I got close to would leave me anyway I had earned a new name with my family the "victim"

What else could they expect from me was I supposed to be happy and cheerful or maybe they just didn't want me or my burden around? I hated myself and couldn't stand my reflection, in the mirror I noticed I started gaining weight what used to be a slender body with my hip bones sticking out, became just flab. But still I didn't care why should I

No-one took notice of me and that's the way I liked it. No-one could ever comprehend what it was like for me living in that house having to be made to act like nothing ever happened. Constant flashbacks and memories. Having to sit and pretend that I was a part of the family, when I knew that I wasn't. The deep sensation kept growing day after day, I did not know what it was but it consumed me completely. I started experiencing blind rages to the extent that I screamed at the monster from somewhere finally came the words that I had kept myself from saying my whole life... I HATE YOU I SCREAMED I HATE YOU SO MUCH.

He looked at me with nothing but disgust and screamed back that I deserved it I ran out the back and sat on the steps as soon as my mum came in the room and screamed at the monster I knew that I was blamed for everything it all made sense now it was my fault everything that happened to me was my fault somewhere I must have gone wrong I must have given everyone the right to hurt me and I just couldn't work it out anymore. Why should I have to everyday of my life try to work out why I was so hated? There was no reason and all of a sudden the rage I felt turned to something completely different that I did not expect I began to cry! I cried and cried and cried I hadn't let myself cry for such a long time and I didn't understand why I was reduced to weakness that would not stop.

My mum came outside and just looked at me with tears in her own eyes, the words she said to me were, "He didn't mean it Faith. You know it wasn't your fault, but you have to stop playing the victim". Victim is that what I was? How could stopping myself from loving and being hurt by anyone be playing the victim?

Days passed and I was in a daze, all I wanted to do was sleep and nothing was helping. I felt nothing but hurt, the more I tried to get rid of it the more I felt it I thought I had stopped myself from feeling this. I couldn't bare anymore I just wanted to die. I felt like I did years before I couldn't do it anymore. If GOD wanted me to go through this then he could kiss my ass. I picked up a piece of paper and started to write my mum everything, absolutely, everything I had wanted to say for years! It had all come out and as I wrote I cried what was happening to me I couldn't live in this sadness anymore. I had just finished writing to mum when my brother called me to come downstairs.

I managed to get myself off of my bed and walk into my mums room, she was sitting on bed her eyes red from crying. Why did I have to inflict so much sadness on my mum? I so passionately wanted it to end and I know somehow she would miss me but it would not be so bad. She could mourn and then move on with her life. I could be up there protecting her. I would no longer suffer. What did she have to say to me now my heart was so heavy? My whole body was! I couldn't even think properly so I stood there for maybe 5 mins just staring until she spoke. When she spoke there was so much hurt in her voice. As she spoke the words "Faith you can't live here anymore, I can't help you I've tried and your aunty Robin can help you more than I ever could I don't know who you are".

"Well that was obvious" I loved my mum but did she know who I was or what I liked or even that I just wanted to die? She begged me to please give it a go. Maybe she did know that I could not live there anymore? As I went back upstairs I could not believe what I had just heard my own mum was sending me away to a place I did not know. To someone else who wanted to be a mum to me because she couldn't? What was I to do? It was too hard for me to think about and I went to sleep.

When I woke for some reason I had thought maybe I could go away and someone would be able to help me. I found myself fighting the urge to take my life the thought of someone trying to make me love them or even love me struck fear in me and I told myself that I would give it a go. Because it was the way out for me. I would miss my brothers and my family but this was the way, that I would be able to get away and show my mum that I could be better. Away from that evil house, my little brother, Corey was coming for a holiday with me so I was not too scared. But I was sad because I had to leave the people I loved the most. My brothers, my mum and my sisters were not even in the picture, because I wasn't even allowed to get close to them anymore. The day we left to travel to, the place that my aunty and her husband and my cousin lived, mum was at the bus station with me. I knew that she didn't have any other choice and no matter what I loved my mum. I secretly loved her so much she gave me the biggest hug that I'd ever received!

My head started aching and hurting. I was really losing all sense of what was happening. Trying to grasp onto anything that even appeared to be real. It did not help one bit that my very excited, hypoactive brother talked the whole way, but in secret I did not mind. Because I would miss him so much it did not matter how much I really did hate myself and life I could and would never ever hate my brothers. They experienced a lot as well they were so much stronger than me. I didn't know if the boys knew what had happened and why I had to leave them. Why I could not live in that house and why I became what I was they didn't even know Why I had begun to hate as much as I did and that before I left for this trip that I had screamed at my mum. That I hated her and she slapped me for the first time in my life.

My mum had slapped me hard across the face I did not mean to say that to her. I hated her for being with the monster and I hated her for not being able to help and love me. I tried to tell her that but we were both shocked at what happened and it was never spoken about again. The truth was I just didn't understand how she could not love us enough to leave. Maybe if she had of been able to love us then I would of been a different person to what I was and I would not hate so much. It did not matter it had all been done now and I was on a bus to what I feared so much I did not know these people and they would end up hurting me. I knew it and that's why I covered and protected myself so tightly so no-one could get to me what kind of hell was waiting for me after all that was the story of my life. Love wasn't real it never had been and people who lied and made out that they knew and experienced love were kidding themselves.

My aunty Robin was such a different person but in a way a lot like my mum the difference is she tried to love me and talked about love so much and for a while I fell for it and even opened up a little. But then I would completely shut down, because they didn't know me they didn't know the shame and the story I held. I was biding my time and waiting for everything to fall apart. To me it felt like I was meant to be here and that I wasn't my mum's daughter. I was actually Robin's raised by my mum. It was strange and when I thought these things for a while I would believe that I was crazy that I did not know what was real it was all just a big nightmare days faded into nights and it did not matter how hard they pushed I would not let them in and when I realised that they worshiped the so called all mighty GOD and went to church I angered so much the fury started coming back. I despised being in church and having to pretend I loved GOD and that he saved me.

Why did they praise such an unloving uncaring GOD? It was then that I realised they were trying to change me. If my mum and a therapist couldn't then what hope did these people have? I knew it wouldn't take long and it didn't before my uncle started yelling and screaming at me and my aunty pulled away from me. I must have been bad and it really did make me see that it wasn't just my family no-one could love me. I missed my mum so much and to my surprise my mum came up to see me on her own. She was so different, but there was a part of me that worried for my brothers being back with the monster. If I was gone then who was he abusing?

I tried so hard to talk with my mum and one night we went for a walk and what my mum said to me made me cry. She told me that she loved me and that I was here to be away from the monster and that house she told me so much that night and I started to see a different side of my mum, which I had never witnessed. Her biggest fear was that I would be like her! That night when I went to bed I slept all night for the first time in years. I felt happiness inside but that wasn't for too long, because in the morning I woke and it was the same cold mum back. Was this some sort of game that the oh mighty powerful GOD played with me? I was so lost, so confused and so angry the sadness had gone and the anger had replaced it again!

I was packed up and sent back yet again, thrown away! That was it! I really was on my way back to my hell I decided that if there was no light in my life any longer even the fantasies I would escape to were gone and phased into nightmares, I could not look at anything and feel happiness. Not even the things that girls were supposed to feel were not there. I had, had enough! This was my life. I could not run or hide from it anymore. I would make sure that I would never again feel. I made a pact with myself that I would never ever again let anyone hurt me! I knew I was worthless and I knew that there was more hurt to come but I would never allow anyone to have my heart. I was back again in the life that was normal for me yet something was different. I wouldn't stand for it any longer I would not let anyone beat me and like hell were they going to see the real me. I didn't even know who the real me was, for too long I had believed that I deserved everything but now something inside snapped!

How dare anyone hurt me I was not a helpless child anymore and if you wanted to hurt me then be expected to have me fight back! I was done with everything it was time to make a stand to make someone listen to me once and For all, I was not staying in that house anymore! I would not be silent any longer! I hated school with a passion but I knew that I could use it to my advantage. My days of being weak were gone. No-one would ever control me again this new sensation I was feeling was a little scary but it made me feel strong for the first time…

CHAPTER 4

The Grass is Greener

It gave me strength and courage, everything that never before had I felt. That afternoon I left the school grounds, to be placed with two lovely older carers. May and Roger. To me they were scary because they were everything I feared. Love and warmth. Just like everyone else, I expected them to give up on me. To my surprise, they didn't. I knew that I wasn't the easiest person to be around, It did not matter what I said or did, they were there for me. And were even able, to get me to go back to school.

I was still made to have visits with my family, just as it had always been. I was the victim, the hypochondriac, the compulsive liar. The one who was always in the wrong the only difference was he Monster wasn't able to physically, hurt me. After having everyone else believing that there was something wrong with me, I expected May and Roger to start believing it. But not once did they. I was safe with them. At home and school I started having problems with my ears. Roger took me into an ear, nose and throat specialist in the city. He examined my ears and I was given a hearing test.

The shock and anger I felt, when the specialist told me, that my ear was damaged and it was from too many repetitive blows to the head. My hearing was only 40 percent. I knew that the monster would get away with it. That he would deny it! With every inch of my being, I knew already, he would never pay for anything he ever did to me as an innocent child and my mum would always be at his side.

It was the monsters great ability to talk his way out of anything and everything. So it really wasn't long at all before the department wanted me to go back. One of the home visits, we went to the beach. I had, had some work done on my ear and my jaw was affected as well. May and Roger had purchased me a special pillow for comfort when I slept and to support my jaw.

The monster was aware that my jaw was very sore and tender; one of the stipulations from the doctor was to chew at least as possible. So what did the monster do? He cooked me a big piece of steak and made me sit and chew it till it was all gone. The tears ran down my face, I wasn't sad I was angry, I hated the man and everything he stood for! I was in pain not only from jaw and ear, My soul was was in pain. He couldn't even talk to me like I had a right to live. Alway's intimidating me without trying. If only it was all lies and I did have a diagnosed mental illness. I had been diagnosed by my therapist. Post-Traumatic Stress Disorder, high anxiety, and depression. But to me that wasn't an illness.

It was never going to stop; if it hadn't up to this point then I knew it never would. I had to now find a way to never return. My mind began to go frantic with worry, as I went through different scenarios in my mind. I didn't realise though my prayers would be answered, I wasn't praying to GOD though, I was praying to any force that would take me away from the existence I lived. It just happened that I ran into an old best friend, beccy.

She wouldn't know it at the time but Beccy and her father were my saviours. They helped me escape the uncertain future I had, in going back. And they found the one person I longed for all of my life. My Dad. May and Roger knew I was not returning and I didn't want them to get into trouble, so I kept them out of everything.

My escape was all so very quick and the night came when I gave May and Roger the warmest cuddle I was ever able to give as I prepared myself for the unknown. That's what it was to me. The Unknown. I didn't know the man I called my father, the only memory I had left me as a confused three year old.

All of the emotions churning inside my stomach were making me a lot more anxious than normal. As their car pulled up and he got out. He wasn't what I had expected or anything like the vision I had made up in my mind. He was a very big man. But when he tried to embrace me, his cuddle was of a stranger. It wasn't warm or inviting, it was strange, to me. Maybe it was me; I was after all in shock.

My heart beating so fast in my chest, I couldn't help but notice the lady standing next to my father. She had more make up on her face than I had ever seen on anyone. I didn't know it then but it was to hide the ugliness. It was all very surreal leaving the only people in my whole entire life, that I felt safe with and allowed myself in my own way, to care for them. I was going with my dad, something I had dreamed about for years. As long as I could remember! But I was also saying good bye to my friend Beccy. She was leaving as well to move to Sydney and I would never see her again. Everything was changing, but I wasn't aware of just how much.

With all of that going through my head, my Mum came up, she had never spoken to me about my father, it was like he had never existed. But I was too caught up in my own relief, excitement and anxiety, which I would never again have to go back. For years my own mother had been too weak of a person to fight for us. To love and protect us. It was very clear that she would never leave him. The monster had destroyed anything beautiful in her! I wouldn't let her get to me anymore. I had always had the unique ability, to block things out completely that were too hard for me to understand and live with.

In the car that night, all I heard was mumbling, I knew I was being spoken to but I was miles away in my thoughts. Was my future paved with misery, as much as what I already experienced and lived through, or was the grass truly greener.

I let myself feel a bit of hope on the drive to my dad's house. I was safe away from the monster and my mum's confusing personality. I vaguely heard Carol asking about all of the wrong doing and the department. She didn't have a clue about all of the abuse and torment. It didn't matter if I only ever told a small taste of what really happened all of those years, because he would always get away with it and my mom was never there to rescue us. Only when she would feel it was to the extreme. Carol seemed beautiful and caring, but in no time at all, I would get the cold hard slap of reality thrust upon me. I was to learn the grass is never greener. It was just an illusion.

My dad was excited and reminiscing about the past. I didn't have too much to remember, because he left before I reached two years of age. A distant and fuzzy memory came to me, of my dad calling me Munchkin. And then it was gone. As we pulled into the drive way this was it. The new chapter. A beginning with my dad. I couldn't love him straight away because I didn't know him and I was still protecting myself. It was all so very strange to me and it took a while to get used to. Especially when I was asked to call Carol my mum. It seemed so easy for them to expect that from me, but it wasn't. I did miss my mum. But every time it came up I wouldn't acknowledge it. I had agreed with myself to try and finally let her go. And after much thought I agreed to call Carol mum, because in the end it was just a word to me.

Carol had three daughters of her own, Jasmine, amy and skye. For a while I tolerated all of them. They were nothing like, my sisters, Sarah and Stephanie. But I told myself, that this was my new family and I would grow to love them. Not too much for amy and Skye. Because I realised they were jealous nasty and spiteful little girls. But it was probably expected because they were young. It was Jasmine that I absolutely adored. To me she was the closest to a sister that I ever had, but unfortunately as she grew up, she changed and turned into her mother, she adored me as well. I had such a soft spot for her, as we spent a lot of time together. But it was when I started seeing everything for what it truly was; it was then that it all changed.

Living with dad and Carol, who I now called mum, was the opposite from what we had experienced with family and friends growing up. There was always, family and friends over or staying with us. I met all my dad's siblings and all of my cousins. They were so caring. Aunty daphne and Uncle Josh were my absolute favourite. In my mum's home we only ever had occasional visits, by the monsters sister who I knew as, Aunty Gene. And any friendships would not last long.

My Mum contacted the federal police to have me taken back. Luckily for me, I was now old enough to choose where I wanted to live. There was no way in hell I was going back. I did miss my mum, as much as I did not want to acknowledge it. But she would not allow that monster to destroy me any longer. There was still hope for me. He may have taken all of my mum's light away but he wasn't going to do it to me. I had wised up in a way, because I realised I didn't have to be brutally punished and put down every day of my life. I was in my dad's care. He saved me and loved me as a dad should. I adored it when he called me daughter and we would always make me laugh, he would let me do thing that I would never have been able to do. He was my hero.

The department, again got involved. What did that organization want from me? When I was put in the too hard basket all of my life. What were they going to achieve? With me telling them everything and why wouldn't anyone let me escape it. Every time I had to tell someone, only small bits, of my horror story, I relived it like it had just happened. It seemed to me that everyone enjoyed my suffering. It really wasn't long before I realized that the evil step mum in the fairy tales was actually true.

It started with witnessing Carol's rages that would be blamed on her ex-husband; countless times she would tell me that Johnathen, her ex-husband, put her head through all the walls in her house. I guess in her own way it was her excuse, for the abuse that would escalate time after time. She went from my dad, to me, even if she abused me physically, it wasn't anything the monster hadn't inflicted upon me. It was always someone else fault that she would fly into a rage. My dad worked as a security guard and was gone long hours. He was the reason I stayed and put up with it. I hardly got to see him so the times I did, I cherished them. I would iron his work clothes and anything I could do for him, because I couldn't show affection. So that was my way I would express it. I knew it wouldn't be long, that I was made to go to school.

I was smoking when I moved with dad, he knew full well that I smoked, so when I said that I would quit he was adamant that I wouldn't start again. I agreed because I really did want to, but it wasn't as easy as what I thought. I was trying to do everything and anything to make him happy. That even though I was overly anxious about school, and being around people to the point I started hyperventilating, I still agreed. I would not let anyone see me at these times. It would feel like my heart, was going to beat out of my chest and the pain in my chest at times made me feel, I was having a heart attack. The pain was unbearable, it didn't matter how much I wanted to calm down, my body wouldn't let me.

I tried to explain to my dad, what was going on inside of me, but he just wouldn't listen or understand. So the first day at school, after my initial appointment to enrol, finding out regardless how many years of schooling I missed, either being too bruised, sick or having to stay home and clean, they were still putting me into year nine. I didn't want to go school; I didn't know anyone and didn't want to. I was fourteen years old about to turn fifteen but I looked eighteen.

The first day they dropped me off, I watched the car drive away and I walked the opposite direction from the school. found a tunnel that became my school for the next two weeks. I would sit in the tunnel for an hour or so, smoking and then go for a walk. I knew I wasn't like other teenagers, I didn't want to go and hang around the shops, I just wanted to be by myself. I was still trying to grasp what was happening in my life, it was as though they all wanted me to act like I had always been there.

One of the things that was haunting me in my mind, was that I had opened up to my dad just a small bit about the molestation. I was shocked and destroyed when he bluntly told me that Frank had been a good friend of his and he just didn't believe it. It wasn't a statement of shock; he was telling me that he didn't believe me. That it never happened! It was this statement from my father's mouth that had me sitting by myself asking for something to happen. I couldn't feel anything again.

Little did I know, my days doing this were numbered, because the school had been in contact with my father asking if I was okay? Because I hadn't showed up at all for two weeks and they had marked me absent. Did my father not care that I was diagnosed PTSD, high anxiety and depression? This was really too much for me. But why should it have bothered me? When nothing had taken this misery away from me, my dad and the principal thought they had come up with the perfect punishment, but really for me it was the total opposite it. My dad sat in my English class in his security uniform, with the students thinking I was a badass, Secretly I was smiling inside, having my dad there with me, was a big comfort. He helped me find the courage that I didn't think I had. I couldn't care less what anyone thought, but to my surprise, that day I made friends. And from that day on I was at school and my found myself loving every subject other than maths. I absolutely enjoyed drama and home economics.

I now had great friends and was going to school every day, home life was good, if there was any abuse, I would shut my mouth knowing I preferred living my life there. There were a few hurdles but that was the reoccurring story that was my life.

I spent most of my time, with Carol. As my dad would literally, work or sleep. I didn't mind her too much, she was an amazing cook and when she wasn't screaming or raging, she tried to be in my eyes, a good step mum. I was taught to cook and take pride in myself as a teenage girl. Something my mum had never done with me. It was the monster, who first told my mum to go and buy my first bra. I was never allowed to put make up on or anything that made me look attractive but it wasn't my mum's fault. Truthfully I didn't care about my image and my body, was only for the brutal pleasure of others.

Living with Carol, someone who always wore make up, smelt beautiful and had nice things, I was bound to start, taking notice of my body. For years I believed I was an ugly duckling. I started losing weight and enjoyed wearing brand new clothing. I wasn't an awkward ugly person anymore. I was actually very voluptuous with curves in all the right places. I should have realized the moment I became aware of my womanly figure that men would also. What I didn't expect was the extra attention Carol's own father who went by the nickname of bully gave me.

I thought the attention was him being a Grandfather as I had never experienced one growing up. To me my body was just a body. As long as no one ever knew, or reached my heart. It started with, taking me places and subtle little touches, finding dirty magazines on his car seat, when I would get in the car. He was grooming me, but I was too stubborn to admit that to myself. I didn't want to know, because it couldn't happen again. But it was when he was able to get me away from home on an overnight trip much to my objection, he wasn't silly. He knew I was wanting my independence and to leave, just waiting to become an adult. Because the moment I became an adult, I could rule my own world. It was this, which he used to his advantage when he fed me alcohol and consequently I was intoxicated. The dirty old man took my clothes off and inserted himself into me. I was not able to think straight and felt sick. Sick from the alcohol and sick from his horrible old body on top of mine. it was all beyond my control.

He left me feeling ashamed of myself and again of what I had allowed happen to me. I couldn't tell my dad and he confirmed that for me, when he stated, quite firmly if I ever told anyone what had happened and what was going to continue happening, that he would have to be tortured and it would be taken to the grave with him. That I wanted it and dad and Carol would believe him over me. Because they already had their own thoughts about me. It happened time and time again. It wasn't normal and for a really unbelievable reason, as much as I tried to do everything in my power to not put myself in that position, I would always end up there. I do not know how. It was a sick joke, Bully, began to give me money and more than once would take me to a sleazy motel. Have his way with me and leave me hating myself more and more, for not having the courage to say anything to anyone. Who would believe me after being sexually abused time and time again?

I hated the dirty perverted man, even more when he started talking about the young girl who lived across the road. That was when I completely gave him everything he wanted. Anything to stop that young girl's innocence being taken. He was a paedophile. It disgusted me. I was already damaged. So if I had to give myself to save another's soul, that's what I would do. It was destroying me. I was old enough to know better, but who would believe that sexual abuse had happened to me, all through my life through three different perpetrators, older men using my body?

Things at school were not going good for me. I was being called a slut, when never once had I been kissed by a boy. I would not allow anyone to kiss me. I did not go to their school parties or anything at all, that would provoke the name calling. 'When I was approached, by boys my age and older, I really was not interested. I couldn't understand why they would call me names when I wouldn't sleep with them. If only people knew the truth about me and all the horrible things I had allowed happen to me. It was to my surprise though, that only a short time later I did start wanting a boy to love me. To kiss me the way I wanted, to hold me and look after me.

It was around my birthday, I began to realise, I was ashamed of myself for even feeling that way, after all I had inflicted onto myself. My soul, had been wounded there were two men in my entire life that did not hurt me or my body. That was my father and my Uncle Josh the big teddy bear. I felt comfortable, safe and trusted my uncle. He knew I smoked regardless of what my dad and Carol had to say. If I didn't have the money for them, Uncle Josh would help me out with a couple. It was a year of living, with this family after missing my brothers, for so long, my dream came true, when my younger brother Corey and older brother Shaun came to live with us within months of each other.

I loved my brothers and nothing could, or would change that. No matter what. I was proud of them, because they had escaped the monster as well. My dad and Carol started saying my brothers had disabilities and were apparently diagnosed with learning disabilities. Corey was put on Ritalin for ADHD and Shaun was sent to a special school. I knew they were different, but to me there was nothing wrong with them, they were my beautiful brothers. It was when they moved in, everything suddenly changed.

Carol started to get a lot more violent, it would escalate, when she began beating into my brothers. It was quite disgusting because they too, were expected to call her mum. Many times I sat and watched, her daughters, playing games with my brothers. They were such manipulating, cunning and nasty little girls. You could see, they enjoyed every moment of it. All of the lies, and false accusations, so many thrown around. It was not only my brothers, I had witnessed Carol throwing glass ashtray's at my father's head. And constantly hitting into him.

She was far from a small lady, so when it came to throwing her weight around, it was easy for her to do. I saw that Carol had such an ugly face, she truly was a snake. A chameleon that was able to camouflage herself. Not only that, she was so good at being fake. So many times I witnessed, her change, from sweet and loving, to psychotic and violent. Literally spitting her venom.

My brother Shaun was not a small helpless boy anymore. His physical appearance had become much like our dad's. He was big and bulky. One day Carol was beating into him, he literally snapped her arm just from his strength. Carol of course, would proclaim he did intentionally. But like always, I was there to see everything. In truth it was from her own rage, all my brother had to do, was grab her arm and hold it, as she flew into a fury. Thankfully I was able to escape the chaos; I had employment at a fruit shop. My first job and I loved it.

I started working at the back of the shop and stacking shelves; I enjoyed being away from everyone, even better I was earning my own money. I could buy anything I wanted and I had my independence. I felt great being my own person and leaving the crap behind me, when I was at work. In time I was asked to work the register. I was afraid and unsure at first, but considered myself lucky, to have a lovely Philippino Lady; teach me with such compassion and understanding. She made it so easy for me, to learn and gain confidence. I wasn't hiding in the background anymore and became one of the best employees. I enjoyed talking to people and was very fast at what I did.

I worked for an Australian man, his name Bob. It was well known at work, that he had one wife and two mistresses. It was a family run business. I was the only one not related. Most shifts on weekends I would close up. The only times, that I did not enjoy, were when, Carol came in and I had to put trollies of product through without her paying. If I didn't, I knew I would have to pay. Doing that and being dishonest, was actually keeping me safe.

After working there for a couple of months, I started noticing, that I enjoyed the company of one of the other employees. He was in his twenties; we would continuously flirt with each other. I wasn't sure, if he liked me in the same way. But it wasn't a long period of time, before it was confirmed. One afternoon, on a closing shift, I had somewhere to go straight after work. I planned to get changed, and freshen up out the back. I knew I looked amazing, in my dress with ample cleavage, with my face done up in makeup. I felt really good about myself, I didn't expect that Wayne, the employee, would take notice. So when I heard a whistle and him say, "Damn you scrub up well".

I somehow, ended up in the back room, as he cornered me and we had sex. It wasn't like all the other times I imagined, that I would give myself away to someone, when I wasn't forced. We did not kiss and I was bent over a bench. As he took me from behind. I became quite good at making moaning noises, and pretended to have an orgasm. So that's what I did to make it finish quicker. I wasn't enjoying it at all. This really was all that men wanted from me. And as long as they did not take my heart, or soul, I would give it to them. That day, I realised that I did not enjoy sex. Why was it so hard, for a man to love me and not use my body for his own pleasure? I had lost all faith that it could or would, ever happen.

Everything at home had completely spun out of my control. The less time I spent at home, the better I was. The father, that I looked up to and cherished, had changed and my perception of him was fading away. I was not prepared for the yet another man I trusted to Unexpectedly leave me paralysed, in shock and disbelief. I was at home in the kitchen, the day that this occurred. Carol had come in and accused me of stealing my Uncle Joshes smokes, but of course I hadn't. I never had the guts to steal anything other than, the groceries at the fruit shop for my own wellbeing.

Uncle Josh was in the room, I looked over at him and he just sat there with his arms crossed. Why didn't he tell her that I would never steal from him? Was I really that worthless to him? I was too busy trying to comprehend what was going on, that I did not contemplate, what was about to happen. My dad was nowhere to be seen and all I could hear was Carol screaming at me, that she knew I took the smokes. So if I was that cunning, that I would sit and she would make me smoke a whole pack of fifty, one after the other! Why was this happening, why did I deserve this? Especially when I had actually not had a smoke, in months. So what else could I do, other than take the smoke that was forced into my mouth and start smoking it? One by one, I smoked the cigarettes; all the while I was being slapped in the face, poked and belittled. But that wasn't enough for Carol, I knew I hadn't done it but it was too late by now, that evil snake had returned. I could feel her rage, and that's when she began hitting into me. And threw me off the stool I was sitting on. Began kicking me hard, blow after blow in the head, in my ribs and in my side. That wasn't all.

I managed to scramble and get up, and try to get away, but she grabbed me by the hair, and pulled me back towards her. I had one chance, so I punched her in the stomach, to try and get away. I thought I had, but she came after me with a broom, not only did she hit me with it, but she began stabbing me. I had never seen her infuriated like this and it terrified me! Because unlike everyone else, she just wouldn't stop and it got worse. My body was so sore, aching, in pain. I felt so sick from the smokes, my heart was beating so hard in my chest, I truly could not understand what was happening and why? Just like every other time, my head hurting, my body shaking I would be out of my body, watching how awful, and unloving humans were.

Witnessing the occurring theme of my miserable existence. This time I did not want to go back down into my body, but it was too late, suddenly I was there! Tasting the blood in my mouth and my swollen face, my aching ribs and the lumps on my head, where my hair had been ripped out. And I had been hit blow after blow! It was only when, my uncle Josh said the words that is enough, that it stopped. I couldn't believe it. Tears were falling but they were not tears of pain, they were tears of rage. Why wouldn't anyone just kill me? I wanted to be dead, as far back as what I could remember. What really was enough, to all the cruel unloving humans? What kind of planet did I live on? Why did I deserve to be hurt and why did everyone hurt me? It was confirmed for me I couldn't trust anyone, and certainly couldn't have faith in anything. All of these thoughts, in my mind, devastated by the cruelty of humanity. I had to get away.

Lying in bed that night, I refused to cry, I knew my soul wanted to but I would not allow it. Sleep was not on my mind, escape was. So in the morning, when it was still dark, I got up from that bed with only the clothes I was wearing, and I walked out that front door without turning back. I did not care anymore, why should I? To hell with everyone! I didn't know where I was going, but my heart certainly did. I was walking towards my old home. If I saw a red car, that looked like Carol's, I would duck behind something and hide. For long hours I walked, it was becoming afternoon. At the next train station, I jumped on the train, to end up at the station the words clearly on the sign, Sandgate.

I didn't know why, but my feet were taking me, towards the hell that I came from. My feet may have taken me there, but I walked straight past the house. I didn't have a clue where I was going, or what I was going to do, no faith at all. All of my life, the sick jokes and games that GOD loved playing with me. It was funny how things worked out because I literally, walked into an old friend, Chanelle, I knew from foster care. And she knew of somewhere I could stay. It was a small little unit; she led me into a little room with a mattress on the floor. I didn't care; it was good enough for me. Because I was so physically and mentally drained and it was because of this, the moment my head hit the pillow and my body found rest. I fell asleep instantly.

I wasn't sure how long I slept, but I was woken by muffled voices in the little lounge area. It was two guys and Chantelle. The guy with long hair introduced himself as Quinton. He was Chanelle's flat mate. I wasn't aware that Chantelle liked him more then what she had said, how could I, after not seeing her for years Until nights later when I went to a party, the first time I tasted beer and wine and was drunk from my own doing.

Chanelle was a lot bigger than me, that night, I laid down on the trampoline, my ribs still so sore, from the beating I had endured, and then suddenly Chanelle fell on me. I was in agony, intoxicated, holding my ribs; I just wanted somewhere to lay where I was safe. I found a bedroom with a single bed. I laid there for a while, until I heard the door open. My heart jumped and I thought it was going to happen again. I couldn't bear having someone take advantage of my body, But it was Quinton, he did not harm me, and he wanted to find out if I was okay. He saw me crying. I couldn't help it. The darkness didn't hide anything. He gave me a hug and laid down and held me.

Not once did he try to force me to do anything, my friendship with Chanelle, was beginning to sour and my friendship with Quinton, was beginning to blossom. It did not take long, before we were officially together! He was twenty one and I was turning fifteen. I was infatuated with him. Especially when he kissed me for the first time. It was everything that I had hoped for, but yet something was missing and when we had sex, I was not pleased. I was left wanting him, to get off me. I felt sick and angry, but he never did anything wrong. It was hard for me to understand. Why? being the first man that I wanted to sleep with and be with, that it made me feel disgusting. And that he was raping me just like everyone else. It just so happened, that Quinton, was getting a place of his own and asked me to come with him. Chanelle had turned nasty towards me; it wasn't really an option that I could, dismiss.

We did not have much, but it didn't matter because we had each other. Even with everything being new, different and actually nice something kept telling me, an uneasy feeling, not to relax or even for one minute. Feel safe. I should have, trusted that feeling because my days were numbered. Chanelle had been very spiteful and I hadn't realised that she was angry with Quinton or that she would find my father's number and consequently one night when I opened our door, there was Carol and dad. With such speed and force, Carol grabbed my hair and dragged me out to the car, but I was fighting and screaming this time. I wasn't going back; I thought Quinton would have done something. But nothing, he stood at the door and watched them push me into the car and drive away. It may have been his shock or better yet, the lies that came from my Dad's and Carol's mouth. Whatever it was I never saw him again. And four years later, found out he had died.

I couldn't do anything there was no escape, the thought crossed my mind that I could open my door and jump out, Then no one could have me. I sat in the back of that car, astounded, by Carol's cruel, unkind, and apparently loving ways. I had only been missing for a few weeks; it was the fear that made me stay. I had no other option and nowhere to go. If they found me once, they would have been able to do it again. This was my life and I would make it the best I possible could with what I had been dealt.

My sixteenth birthday was coming up, I told my dad all I wanted, was The Movie Dirty Dancing. Because as a child, I would imagine I was that girl. Things weren't as bad, or so I thought. My best friend Natasha was in love with my brother, Shaun and was always coming over. I myself could only stand her in small doses, she wasn't the best person, I would watch in utter amazement as she sucked up to Carol. Anything she could do, to squeeze into my reality. I had the feeling she wanted my life, and was trying to be me. The times I witnessed this, I would wonder to myself why would she want to be me? When I had spent years wanting to be anyone other than who I was.

My dad and Carol were both working, dad long hours doing his security, and Carol had wormed her way into the fruit shop. I had to give her credit, she really was good at that, her ability to change at the snap of your fingers, able to fit in and play the role of anyone. But the story was different at home. Behind the closed doors, the real Carol would be out. Not able to hide, behind a façade and a face full of makeup. It wasn't really a surprise when her daughters grew into the same thing. They must have thought packing makeup onto their faces would hide what they truly were inside. Nasty jealous little girls. Carol really didn't deserve all of the blame because my questions were answered the moment I met her mother.

They all treated my brothers like idiots and dirt beneath their feet. But when they would easily manipulate situations and even my father. I began to realize, that they held no beauty within. They may have been beautiful on the outside but certainly not on the inside. Doing whatever it took to get whatever they wanted. Even Jasmine, the once young girl I had adored.

CHAPTER 5

Darkness Prevails

One of the memories that would haunt me and make me wish, for years that it never occurred, was the dark day that I met Blake lawson. I had just gotten home from school angry and disappointed, with my dad, because yet again he'd let me down. I wanted him there, to see me receive an award that I had proudly earned. I knew he was on the computer; my father's life consisted of work, sleep and the computer. There wasn't much said because it wasn't unusual to me. I was angry at myself, for even thinking, that he would have been there. I slammed his door and stormed out of the room. I could hear voices, one was my brothers and the other was a New Zealand accent. The words spoken were: "Whoa who is that chick?"

And my brother Shaun's reply was, "That's my sister Faith, watch out she is feisty". I wasn't too bothered as I had things to do. I walked into the kitchen to get dinner ready and standing there in front of me was a bright, blue eyed guy, with jeans falling down his backside. The only words he had the hide to speak to me where: "Cook me some eggs." I looked at him with disgust. Who the hell was this wannabe?

My reply was: "Excuse me? Cook your own damn eggs." Because by this time I had my own cruel share of men and boys. I walked out of the kitchen to go shower. I had to get dinner ready and iron dad's clothes. I knew it was in the shower I would settle down. My fights with my dad were never physical and I wasn't able to stay mad at him for long. I found out later, from my brother, that the guy's name was Blake. I could not stand him

Unfortunately he lived just round the corner and his visits became regular. I tried to hide the fact that his piercing blue eyes and accent attracted me. So much so I found myself flirting with him and mucking around. I was never going to sleep with him as I could never stand his attitude or his mentality. Just his eyes and accent. But he started paying me lots of attention and before too long, I found myself under a blanket more than once fooling around with him. My dad could not stand him either. After going out to parties and hooking up with girls, he would always end up at my home with me. I was his little piece on the side. Not as attractive as his usual preference. Because under no extent was he ugly.

Our fooling around went on for months, until one night Carol thought she caught us having sex on the lounge. At this time we were not doing anything of the sort. It did not matter to my father, a week later when Carol wanted to be spiteful and told him we had, had sex. I hated the woman with such a passion, for what she did to me, my brothers and my father. For what her perverted father did to me, for pretending she was something wonderful and hiding her true colours from everyone else. I hadn't had sex with Blake and I tried to tell my dad and make him believe me.

I didn't care what Carol did to me, but it was my father, the last person, I had put all my trust into, to protect and love me as much as possible and it was my father that destroyed me. As much as anyone else ever had. All of a sudden he started screaming at me, and calling me a slut like my mother. He grabbed me and held me as Carol started hitting into me. I didn't know what I did to provoke the brutal attack from both of them. I didn't sleep with Blake, I was being thrown around, kicked and my hair was being ripped from my head in many places. I was literally being thrown around the room, slammed into walls, the floor and dragged up by my hair. At one stage Carol dragged me into her personal bathroom and slammed my head into the toilet bowl.

I'd given up on fighting, there was no point. Whenever I fought back, I was always beaten harder. She picked me up from the toilet bowl, slammed me into the basin, and was punching me in the head, all the while calling me every name you could think of. That wasn't it though. They hadn't finished! My dad grabbed me up from the floor and threw me onto their bed. His heavy body on top of mine so I could not move. My head was dangling over the side of the bed, while my body was being squashed. I was suffocating, with his weight on top of me. What was he going to do?

My question was answered when my father, put his hands around my neck, and squeezed. I couldn't breathe, because his hands were so tight. This was it. My own father, the only person left, I trusted to never hurt me, was the one that was going to take my life. Everything blurred, it was almost like slow motion. I looked up and saw a bright golden, white, light, where the ceiling was. I didn't feel any pain; I could see the ugliness in my father's eyes. I realised right at that moment, that he never loved me, no one did. And I was finally going to be set free.

But it wasn't to be, Because I then heard their screaming voices and I could feel all the pain in my body. The tight grip was loosened, Why wasn't he finishing the job? I looked up at him with hate, pure hate and disgust. My body ached more than it could ever remember. But it wasn't just my body. My heart and soul ached, a deep mournful ache.

Why wouldn't anyone just take this away from me? Why wasn't I released from this hell that I lived every day? Was I just here to be a punching bag, a body for men to rape and be beaten over and over again? There must have been something about me that made everyone I had ever trusted and even loved in my own way, beat me, degrade me, use me and throw me away like a worthless piece of rubbish. I knew that I was being screamed at but I blocked it out. I could not hear what they were saying that was until I heard the words that came out of my father's mouth snapped me out of it. He had said "If you want to be a slut like your mother, then I will take you back there".

I felt the tears pouring from my eyes and the pain my body was in but nothing else. There were no feelings at all. I heard my self say in a numbed tone, "Good". Even my brother Shaun had turned against me. Something I never thought would for one second happen. Dad and Shaun took me out to the car with just the clothes on my back. I was shoved into the back seat. My brother leaned his seat against me so I couldn't move even if I tried. I was beyond shock. This man, my own father, was screaming he was going to take me out to the bush and beat the shit out of me and leave me for dead! I wanted them all to hurt as much as I did. Could any of them feel the pain or misery that was inside of me?

An unspeakable sensation was growing more as each day went by. I couldn't name it because it was nothing; I couldn't feel any emotion other than misery or anger and even that was fading away fast. I wanted and needed my mum. I was so scared I would be refused and rejected. They drove me all the way to Sandagate and without any hesitation got me out of the car, and drove off without a second glance. I was left standing across the road, from the unknown yet again.

I managed to find my way over to the front door. My body was shaking and I wanted to sleep. It was late afternoon, but it wasn't just that I wanted to sleep. I wanted to sleep and never wake up. So weak I couldn't stand it any longer. I knocked on the front door and when it opened, standing there in front of me, was the monster. I heard myself ask for my Mum. I was crying as it was all too much for me. He told me go upstairs and that he would have to go speak to my mum. Every step I took, the memories came flooding back to me. I really needed to go to sleep. I needed my mum, to hold me, so I could say goodbye. I wasn't meant to die without seeing her one last time. My step dad's voice interrupted my thoughts. How could I call him the monster when there were so many other monsters in the story of my life. He called me downstairs and as I entered the room, my mum was sitting there. She asked me what had happened. I managed to tell her, as much as I could it was not everything, and then she told me we were going to the police station. I had to have photos taken of my injuries, my bruised and battered body, but what were the police going to do?

Never had they helped in the past, I was beyond caring. I tried as much as possible to fit back in and I was relieved to be with my older brother Wayne and my two younger sisters, Sarah and Stephanie. But they had grown up and changed beyond my comprehension. The feeling always there, that I didn't belong anywhere. Nothing was as it used to be, my step dad, was not physically abusive anymore. Yet still very intimidating and controlling. My whole family had changed as there was no abuse and I couldn't understand, why? Why did I have to be beaten and abused and the others did not?

Couldn't it be like that with our whole family together? Why all the pain and sorrow? Not only had my siblings changed, I did not recognise my own mother. She now had piercings and a tattoo. Mum would hide her own pain and sorrow, by trying to make light of situations. It was voiced and quite clear to me, that I was the blame for everything that went wrong. I wore that blame on my chest. If I hadn't been born everything that had happened would not have. It did not matter how good things seemed, or how well I could put a smile on my face and tell myself everything was fine. there was something horribly wrong inside of me. What I felt was emptiness. Nothing took it away.

I tried to talk to my mum I tried to tell her I felt so empty. But the words would never come, I tried so hard to shake the feeling but it hung over me like a black cloud. Something was missing inside of me. I truly did not want to live anymore. If no one would take me out of this existence, then I would set myself free. I watched my mum taking tablets all of my life and I knew there were boxes of all different types in her medicine box downstairs. It wasn't a spur of the moment decision. I knew I was about to take my life. I thought about it for days and nothing else.

I needed to tell my mum and explain everything. I could not speak about deep things, I could only write, so that is what I did. I wrote her a letter to tell her how sorry I was for everything, that I could not live anymore. I could not deal with myself that I hated everything I was. Everything that I stood for, I couldn't stand seeing my reflection. Everything in my heart that I could possibly explain, I put it in the letter. That letter was to become my suicide letter. It wasn't long after that the perfect day and time finally came for me to be set free.

mum and my step dad had gone out and left the girls at home. What may have seemed selfish to others, about taking my life near my sisters, was a sweet sort of comfort to me. I loved my sisters as much as I tried to love everyone, who meant something to me. I tried to let things go with my step dad, but I could not let go or forgive, the brutal punishments and torment he inflicted on me as a child and teenager. How could I? My bed was a mattress in the lounge room upstairs. I could have just slit my wrists or poisoned myself. But I had suffered enough in this lifetime. I deserved to die peacefully. I walked downstairs into the kitchenette, took the basket out of the medicine cupboard. I swallowed handfuls of tablets, as many as possible. The more I took, the quicker they would work. It was strange how happy and relieved I was knowing I was going to die.

I didn't know how long it would take so I went back upstairs to watch some television, until I began to feel very drowsy and not so good. I must have passed out for a little while, because I tried to open my heavy eyes. I could hear my little sister Stephanie asking me if I was okay. I managed to mumble I wasn't feeling okay. This was the way I chose to end my life, so I had to bare it.

The next time I was coherent, I was being slapped in the face by my mum's friend Ruth, who lived across the road. She was telling me I was an idiot and asking what had I taken? That mum would kill her if I died. I managed to slur the words; I don't want to be here just leave me to die. Ruth panicked as I passed out again. In and out of consciousness I could feel I was in a car, moving, going somewhere, but I couldn't open my eyes or really make sense of anything, other than the need to sleep and never wake up. I didn't want to get better, just please let me go, that's all I wanted.

I could feel myself slipping away, like a dream, it was all a dream. Life was the nightmare, death the goal. I wasn't in my body; I was in an amazing space. I did not recall ever feeling such a joy within my whole being. Unconditional love. There was no pain; only peace. A feeling of wholeness, beautiful white golden, light. Standing there before me, was the most glorious Angel, her hair golden, her eyes bright blue, with the most spectacular wings.

I was not scared. On the contrary, the feeling I had was the feeling of belonging with her. When she spoke it was the most beautiful sound I had ever heard, like music to my ears, she was there to deliver a message to me. The message that I had to return to finish my journey, Through me others would heal their suffering andThrough my suffering, would come wisdom, strength and power. She told me I must learn to love to remember who I really was. She was then gone, I felt myself being pulled back from that magical space. The pain and suffering again I could feel, so deep in the core of my being. That place and message lost for long years. I would not remember any of it until I was of twenty nine years of age. I opened my eyes, to my mum sitting beside me.

Her eyes red and face wet with tears, in her hand she held my letter, I looked at her with eyes of pain. My mother said to me: "Why could it not be her?" It wasn't my mum that I wanted to die, it was me. I couldn't hide it this time, from anyone, they all knew what I had done, and by the letter what was really going on inside of me, as much as I was able to describe and explain it.

I was placed in a psychiatric facility, but what good was that going to do for me? No one could or would, be able to help me feel better. All awareness of that divine experience lost. I was really good at pretending and acting the way people expected and wanted. Maybe that was something I had learned from Carol. So after making it seem I was so much better and apparently fixed, I was released into my mum's care. My mum knew I couldn't live there anymore, she knew too well; I was lost in my own consuming darkness. So when the time came that I told her I had found a shelter I could live at, for the first time in my life she finally let me go.

I had felt completely alone, all my life, even with people around me. But now I was absolutely alone. No one knew who I was nor did they know my past. not able to see the wounded soul that I was. Or the suicidal thoughts that I had lived with. I could now be whoever I wanted. Something I had spent my whole entire life wanting! This was the next chapter of my story.

CHAPTER 6

The New Chapter

When I returned home from the psyche ward, my mum and I had not recovered from what I had done. The words still fresh from my letter, if I wasn't allowed to die, then I would conceal myself and bind myself so well that not a single human would be able to get to me ever again. I didn't realise that when I set that intention, so strongly, with such force in my soul that I was giving my body the orders to create layers of weight.

On the train that afternoon, on my way to the shelter, with all of that in my mind. I couldn't help but to feel anything other than, lost. I had never been in this predicament, even when I had run away, Quinton was at my side. This was so very different that I couldn't help but to cringe at what humanity, had in store for me. What did the future hold? Maybe where I was going there was lost souls, just like me. Who could understand the pain and agony I had lived with? No one not a single soul had ever been able to understand me. All through my life, I would hear what is wrong with you? I just can't understand you? You have issues!

With all of this constantly being drilled into my mind, I started to believe that I was mentally unstable. Did I have an illness that didn't have a name yet? I would often think about it when I found myself telling stories that I made up to people. I didn't care they didn't know me. Anything but the real truth of my horrible existence. I spent hours sometimes making up a fantasy existence in my mind.

It was great and better than the reality I was living, adventurous, smart, funny happy, anything but the truth. Who would want to know about the dark thoughts that clouded my mind? or the extent of consuming suffocating darkness, that had taken over me and my life. I hated everyone and everything. It wasn't so bad, when I moved into the shelter, I did meet other misfits and lost souls.

I began to open myself up just a little bit, that wasn't a good or smart thing for me. I started smoking weed and drinking It didn't take me long to meet friends. I was always better at making friends with guys than I was with women. Just another thing to confuse me. It was man that always had taken my innocence and destroyed me. My friend Joel was different; he was gay and always the life of the party.

Then there was Paul who was the gothic, eventually we hit it off and began to fool around with each other. If I could please them without having to have sex with men, I would because I did not enjoy it. Always getting angry and wanting them to get off of me. I earned the nickname of a cock tease, through wanting to protect my body. I went to two different shelters and got myself into situations that were never good, but I was learning to live. All I wanted to do was get high and drink to not feel what was going on inside of me.

The weed wasn't doing it for me anymore. It was when I had ecstasy for the first time. I didn't feel what I was doing and it was great. The feeling of wanting death would disappear even if it was for just one night. When I wasn't out dancing, I wanted it every day. I wanted to be out of it. Not comprehending what I was doing, I had lost all control off myself. I had the opportunity to move into a house with Josh and his friend. My money was always spent on drugs and alcohol. I was a wreck and I felt I belonged nowhere. After some time, I decided to take the train to see my mum. Always needing to be high. It became very apparent, that I could not do anything unless I had smoked or popped a pill.

One of my visits home, I learned that my brother Wayne was best mates, with two brothers up the road. It was clear that the older brother wanted to sleep with me, after I got to know them a bit better. But it was his younger brother Tristan that I fell for. He was attractive smart and mysterious. I fell harder than I ever felt was possible. When I would visit

I would spend a lot of time flirting with Tristan. There was definitely something there. Such an intense feeling. One day I found myself under Tristan fooling around.

It was awesome and I wasn't feeling scared I wanted him. The first guy I would have willingly given myself to. He sent shivers down my spine and gave me Goosebumps. I wanted him inside of me. The sensation in my body was over powering. But it stopped when his brother would get home. Nothing would come of it. The only guy that I would have opened up for and probably given my whole self. It wasn't just me that Tristan had his eyes on and to my dismay he chose the other girl. I was a mess of intoxication and weed, the devastation of Tristan playing with me hit me harder then I could have anticipated.

I didn't show it, I just felt it. But I came to realise it wasn't about Tristan! It was because he was the first guy I actually wanted and trusted it was as though I was slapped in the face. I couldn't have the man I wanted but it really shouldn't have been a surprise to me, because all through my life, never could I have, anything I would have wanted. I stopped going home for a while, and knew if I stayed at the house with Joel, I would never be able to get better.

I had decided that I needed to live on my own away from everyone, my own home. One of the biggest shocks on one of my home visits was finding out, that my mom too also smoked weed. And not only that but Tristan would come down and spend hours with her, both getting high together. Everything was changing at such a fast pace, I struggled trying to keep up with it all. So when I got my own little unit, I would stay there trying to piece together my own life.

I met some of my neighbours and decided to have a couple of drinks one night; I was getting to know two of the girls in the duplex. But as the night wore on, they disappeared! I usually drank premix drinks, but this night I bought a bottle of rum and was using glasses. So high and enjoying myself, because that was the only time I did. Not thinking something was wrong, I knew the feeling of being drunk, but the feeling I started having was disorientation. I must have fallen asleep because when I awoke very fuzzy, I was in the unit with one of the guys that had visited earlier.

I was not coherent at all! I tried to get up and go to the bathroom, but I was not feeling well. I thought he was helping me but he led me to my bed. I couldn't even speak I was so disorientated. When I came around I was in my room and my clothes were off he was having his way with my body. I was being raped and I couldn't do anything about it. I was violated and taken every way possible. I vaguely recall he was calling me a naughty dirty little slut. His hands all over my body. When he finally finished I could see the sun coming through my windows. I cannot say when he left because I must have fallen asleep again!

When I awoke, there was a sick feeling in my body, bruises between my legs and semen all over my breasts. I could taste the blood in my mouth, every part of my body that could have been violated, was violated and aching. I could not comprehend what had happened or how it happened. Eventually when I could make my way to shower, I collapsed. I am not sure how long I sat in my shower I could not get clean. I kept scrubbing and scrubbing, the disgusting feeling would not leave.

Who could I tell, who would believe that this was a reoccurring theme in my life? Who would ever believe that I had been raped again? I know I did not ask for it. I just had to get over it and bury it deep down. So I couldn't relive it ever again. I don't know how long I stayed in my shower, my head was still woozy, and I had to get back into my bed. I managed to make sure my blinds and doors were locked. I crawled into my bed and cried myself to sleep. I didn't ever tell anyone about that night. I couldn't! And I could not stay there I was scared.

I tried to ask the girls, the next day what had happened? The cruel man, who did that to me, went around boasting that I had wanted it all night. I didn't tell the girls what happened. I was sickened, luckily only a week later, my mum had seen things were going good. So she said I could move back home. I wasn't safe anywhere, so being back there was nothing. My mum was a completely different person, she was smoking joints all of the time. I had never seen her drink alcohol, let alone smoke pot. But she had no worries and wasn't sad. My step dad was always at me about something. It didn't take him long to lash out and hit me in the face. It was time to move out and this time my mum had found me a place.

It was with a friend of theirs, I was able to rent one of his rooms. It was in the same suburb as her and mum was close if I needed anything. I could just ring and she would be there. It was actually great and I got along fine with James. He was never a threat. They would come and visit but I had my own space. I was starting to settle in and get past the rape in my own way. Even the darkness inside of me was starting to settle down. It was always there just not always so consuming, I was so very lonely. So when I met Luke, I thought he was my solution. He was soft, caring and peculiar, nothing at all like the men I had been with.

Somehow we started seeing each other. My mum and step dad could not stand that I was with him and that they had no control over me. After only a few weeks everything was turned upside down and yet again I was rejected. When I was doing everything my family wanted of me, everything was fine and that was the only time. I moved in with Luke and his family because my mum had waved her wand of controlling people and I had nowhere to live. His family were beautiful.

His mum, Sister, Brother and step dad. They all took me in. I knew I wasn't in love with Luke; I was infatuated with someone loving and not hurting me. I was wounded from so much, every time something came up, I would immediately push it straight back down. Nine months flew by with Luke, then I found out I was pregnant. I always wanted someone to love me and love me back. I kept telling myself that I loved Luke. I constantly made myself believe that it was love and I was just being silly and hormonal. But it wasn't. For months I had been telling myself that he didn't hurt me and never would. He looked after me and even loved me.

Was I ever not really confused by my emotions and thoughts? The conflict and suffering had begun to surface again. This was not only my first baby, this was a child, a life, and I needed my mum. I tried to contact her several times over the months, always the same cold and stubborn outcome. Being pregnant with her first born grandchild, I thought that it could be different now. Luke and I had moved out of his families' house into our own little flat. Every doubt I had about our relationship I ignored. I found the courage to ring my mum one last time.

To tell her about the beautiful life that was growing inside of my womb. When she answered the phone, I quickly spoke the words that I needed to say. I wasn't taking notice of what she said to me because no matter what, how hard I tried, my mum was the only one who could break through my walls of protection and hit me straight in the heart, though she never knew this. I was the only one who was able to see her vulnerable side that was hidden away. I didn't realise it was because I did the exact same thing. Mum agreed to come down and meet Luke.

All I knew was that I needed my mum, I was seventeen and pregnant telling myself that I loved the creator of the beautiful little soul, that I so loved already. But who was I kidding? If I left Luke I would be alone. He never hurt me; I knew nothing was ever a fairy tale with my family. Never did I feel a part of them, I never belonged anywhere, not with my mum nor my dad. No matter what there was always an ache in my heart for my mum. When I was near her, I would be reduced to that tiny little girl, aching for her mum's love.

I couldn't understand any of my conflicting, confusing, thoughts and emotions. With so many people in my life, telling me they could never understand me. The real truth was I couldn't understand myself so what hope did the world have? It came as a surprise to me, my mum asked me to move back home with Luke. I knew only too well that he was tolerated. I was being pulled two ways. Luke could not stand them and told me every day that I couldn't see it. That they controlled me like a robot, programed to jump when they said leap. I was too scared to upset anyone. I spent my time making everyone happy and trying to bridge my family and Luke. I wouldn't dare push any boundaries, I found out I was having a little baby boy. And he would be named Jake.

I was stressed out with everything one night; thirty eight weeks pregnant and fell down the stairs. I wasn't too badly hurt, but because of it I was in the early stages of labour the next morning. After a lengthy labour of nineteen hours with no pain relief, my beautiful little man came into the world. I was in shock, holding this tiny innocent little life in my hands.

He had come out blue and for a minute I thought I had lost him. But thankfully he was a miracle lying in my arms. Somewhere inside, I knew he was sent here for me. Nothing else mattered to me other than my amazing child. I was in love, I had just turned eighteen and Luke twenty one. We were first time parents learning everything. I was lucky that my son started sleeping through the night at four weeks old. But my eyes began to open, and become aware of how controlling my family was.

And it wasn't just my step dad, it was my mum. Luke would do as much as he could, but trying to open up to my mum and tell her I didn't love him and something was surfacing again, I was blinded and put everything down to them looking after myself and Jake. But it was far more than that, they had started taking over my role with Jake!

It was all very strange and out of my control, they were literally controlling everything, I couldn't understand why as much as I loved my little man, that I was so unhappy. I was supposed to be a happy first time mom, but it was far from the truth. I hoped so much that the feeling would come. But it never did. I put my smile on, and acted the way everyone expected. All the while I was suffocating. It was all becoming too much. My reality was starting to blur. All the questions I had asked myself all through my life started resurfacing. What was wrong with me? Was I ever going to be happy?

I was smoking again, and even drinking I would not allow myself to get intoxicated. The rape that had happened in my unit had terrified me so I could never feel the feeling of losing self-control again. There was no way. We tried to spend as much time as possible outside of the house, with Luke's family, Until I couldn't stand it any longer. I had been weighing everything up in my mind for weeks. I chose to stay with Luke, and make the best of itand Stay together for our baby, our son.

I didn't love him, but I preferred to live my life with Luke and Jake. I had no strength left to live with and make my family happy. I had become an adult and a parent. It was time for me to look after and raise my son. The day we stood as a united front, and told my family we were leaving, was the last day in years, that I would ever see them again. Thankfully we had left Jake with his Grand Dad and Grand Ma to face the music. I had such a bad feeling, but it had to be done. It wasn't music we were facing. It was drama. I was screamed at and belittled, just as I had been as a child. All of a sudden, I was being pulled by the hair out of the front door by my step dad. He locked it behind me, and I heard him hitting into Luke.

I couldn't believe it; I was in the front yard screaming, what was wrong with these people? I had to ring the police, my mother yelled out to my step dad that we were not worth it and that I was always going to run. There was no charge's laid, we just wanted to get back to our son. For days after, I felt that seeing my brothers and dad after years, was what was missing. Constantly needing to fill the emptiness with someone or something. The day I made the call to my brother Shaun, I didn't know it, but I literally had signed a contract with the darkness, to take over my life, and eliminate all light and hope. If I thought there was no way that my life could get any darker, I was sadly and extremely wrong. It came in the form of a man, his name was Blake Lawson.

The teenage boy that I had, had a crush on, years earlier. The day I ventured back into my dad's life and introduced them all to my beautiful son Jake, Blake happened to be there, maybe it was my sick fate or a funny joke that the dark forces played with me, but I was blinded by it.

CHAPTER 7

A Contract Signed

Luke and I were slipping completely away from each other. Nothing I did could stop it. So that night out the front of my father's house I was having a smoke, when Blake appeared. He walked up to me and bluntly asked, "What was I doing with that guy?" Then proceeded to tell me: "You could do better than that".

I replied to him, "What you?" I laughed at him and walked off. Luke could obviously see the attraction between Blake and I. After a week of trying to fix things, we separated. And instantly Blake started, making him known quite often. Consequently weeks later, he took Luke's place. I knew that I only accepted Blake because I was scared of being alone. The thought of loneliness scared me more than anything. While I was at my dad's house, I met up with an old friend, Natasha from school.

Yet again, more darkness that came, in the form of a person. We had all started spending time together, drinking and doing stupid things. But Jake was always safe. It was only a few weeks later, that we came up with the idea, to get a house together. Natasha and I would sign the lease and my brother Shaun would move in. I loved my brother living with me. I could read people like a book. It was one thing I noticed over the years, even though with all the consuming darkness I held the ability to see through people, even when they were not good for me and I knew that they would hurt me.

I still walked where angels dare not tread. Always tempting fate. Moving into my first house, was supposed to be my new beginning for Jake and I. I was supposed to do the right thing and believe me I tried. When it was my brother, Natasha and I, it was fine. But after only a few days, Blake moved in to help out. And with him he bought along a friend. Yet again reckless abandonment. With the voice in my head telling me to walk away, before it was too late. I blocked it out, and started drinking and partying, in the house.

My brother Shaun didn't like what he was seeing and he would try to have his say. But I didn't care. There was a reckless abandonment and I couldn't fight it. It was so powerful, the need inside of me, and the attraction I had to this life. It was only a week living there, that Blake began to be abusive. He grabbed me around the throat one night, when he was completely intoxicated. And threatened to throw me out the window. That was only the beginning.

I noticed that my money started disappearing. As much as I tried to pay the rent and give Jake a good home. Something wouldn't allow me to do that so I gave in an admitted defeat. I had made contact with my mum again, because I had left Luke and that would have made mum happy. But I refused to listen to what anyone was saying. I just couldn't be alone and I enjoyed drinking and getting drunk because I had nothing else to care about. I knew I had Jake and I did love him. But there was something seriously wrong with me. I couldn't stop what was happening, so I had to ask my mum for help. I asked my mum to look after Jake only for a little while; I could again get my life together. I really did want to do the best thing, but I was too far gone.

A deep depression had come over me and along with it; I started throwing up everything I ate. I noticed the weight was starting to fade away, so conflicted, needing and wanting my son. But knowing I wasn't right for him. Knowing I couldn't have my son back, it didn't matter how many times I begged my mum, and told her that he was my son, she refused, because she had heard from my brother Shaun, who after many years of separation, had reunited and moved back with our mum. In doing so told her everything that had happened in that house. I knew that I was slowly destroying, everything around me. I just did not care. My heart ached for Jake and my family tried everything in their power, to try and keep him and not give him back.

I was allowing Blake and Natasha to take over my life; I gave all my power away and followed everything they were doing. Blake had such an obsession with driving, that we spent many hours in the car. Eventually the friendship with Natasha and I very fast became frosty. Because they both tried to control me, Blake and Natasha despised each other. It could not continue, the real estate was contacted and our lease broken. Natasha left leaving things in a very dark place, I knew she was always jealous of me, but when she told me to my face, I stared at her with disbelief, thinking if only you knew Natasha You would have never had said that.

It was before all of this happened that we had a very distressing car accident. It was exactly two weeks, before I eventually got the courage, to call the police and get my son back. The day of the accident, it had just started pouring, I was in the passenger seat and Jade was driving. In the back was Natasha, and her boyfriend Mike. We had just driven out of Red Rooster, when all of a sudden I could not see the road. My heart went into my stomach when I had asked him to pull over, because the windscreen wipers had stopped working. He yelled at me to shut up. I turned to look out of my side window, all I saw was a flash of green coming straight for me, then a bang, my body was jolted, all I remember was being thrown around. And then, nothing.

I recall opening my eyes and somehow we were upside down. I was on top of Blake, out of nowhere, four big muscled men, with bald heads, came over and one by one, lifted us out of the car. Natasha was screaming, and was a big girl. She was worried that they would not be able to lift her. Everything then became a blur to me. When the shock subsided, the police ambulance and fire brigade were there. I started asking where were the big bald men that rescued us. But no one had known what we were talking about.

The car caught fire, and all of a sudden Blake started screaming as there was petrol can in the back. We were lucky that the fire brigade had put it out., Blake had received most of the injuries. But then I found out, he was the one in the wrong. He had driven through a give way sign, so consequently the lady in the other car had T-Boned us, and rolled the car three times. They all said we were lucky to be alive. That day what opened my eyes, was when I was told, that if Jake had been in the car, he would not have survived. It was that statement that made me fight to have my son back. Unfortunately I was still with Blake.

I couldn't explain it he was like a toxic drug that I could not get enough of. It wasn't long after that that I met his family. His father Kevin was everything you could ever want in a loving father. Yet his mum was the complete opposite. I could see that she despised me, but it was only because of Jake that I was given a chance. I would cringe, whenever she was around. But over the years, when yet again, we had nowhere to go we would end up back under their roof. If I thought my child hood was bad, I had really no idea, of what a six year relationship would do to me.

Constantly homeless, I was always searching for that vision of a white picket fence, and the happy family. I would endure, constant judgedment. I had to teach myself how to be a mum. Sharon, Blake's mom did not help. She would look at me with disgust. I was rejected by everyone I met, whether they were friends or not. Not just Blake's family, but it seemed that everyone was condoning his ways. I wasn't in love with this man, but I had gotten in so deep, that I couldn't find a way out. When Jake was nearly two years old, I found out, I was pregnant. This wasn't what I wanted. How could this have been?

I had made sure I had been completely protected. Maybe this one I could be closer to and love the way I should have with Jake. I held so much guilt, for my son's life and maybe just maybe, I could make up for it with this one. I couldn't forgive myself for the hell I put myself and my son through; Jake had witnessed so much in such a short time, of Blake beating into me. It would never be at his parent's house, I guess that's why they found it so hard to believe. But it was my own fault, I felt like I couldn't leave him because he would get better. And the times I did try to leave, it wasn't long before we were back together again. I cannot lie there were some good times, but they were very rare. I lived my life the way I did, and not a single word that anyone would say, was listened too. Even when I realised I was living with an alcoholic.

When Jake was about twelve months old, Blake had said he was going out with his mate, for a few drinks. I didn't get a say, I chose to stay with this man, so I had to live with my choices. I was left home with his mate's partner, and we were just going to have a quiet night. Blake's mate was a lot like him. I trusted him this night because he would always say sorry and threaten to kill himself if I left him. So it just became a habit. A regular habit.

This night all I asked of him, was to, before he left get some nappies for Jake. Blake didn't work, and for years it was the money I got, that would support us. He would take our rent money and drink it away. He didn't care; I was always left scared of being without a home. That night I waited hours for him, Jake had wet his last nappy; my poor little boy had to wear a tea towel for a nappy. I didn't care what excuse he had this time. I felt like the worse pathetic excuse for a mother. It was early in the morning when I heard him. As expected, intoxicated, stumbling around the back yard. The rage inside of me erupted; I went out the back and screamed at him: "WHERE HAVE YOU BEEN? ALL I ASKED WAS FOR YOU TO GET JAKE SOME NAPPIES!" I couldn't help it, he came towards me, and for a split second I had nerves of steel. My face right up near his, I told him that he was a pathetic excuse, and I was DONE! I thought that he was just going to turn away, but then I saw the rage in his eyes and felt him snap.

I just stood there frozen; and without any thought he head butted me and started punching into my head. I didn't cry, I screamed at him! The more that he laid into me, the more I screamed, until his mate came out of the back door, that's when he snapped back, but it was too late. It was that night, he forced himself onto me after I had refused and said no. I was stuck. I couldn't leave. I had nowhere to go. One of the horrible memories that my son carries, is when he was two and a half and he had walked into the bathroom to see what was happening.

Blake had been drinking with mates and for no reason, started hitting into me, in the bedroom because I had smoked weed, with his mate and gotten completely high. It felt good, just to laugh and feel the weight of the world, lifted from my shoulders. Jake was asleep, in bed, but I was accused of flirting. This is what started another beating. His mate actually tried to stop him, which was the first time, anyone had ever tried to step in and it was because he did like me and I knew that. I was punched numerous times in my bedroom and all through the little cabin we were living in at the time.

I managed to get away and run into the bathroom. I tried to shut the door but he was too strong. He was not a big man but when he snapped, he somehow had super strength. I was cornered, punched and kicked until I was left curled up on the floor, covering my head with my arms. Jake had climbed out of his bed, with his bottle in his hands, and came into the bathroom, Blake went to hit me, elbowed Jake straight in the face and gave him a little black eye. I did not learn from this even when I found out that he had slept with other people. So when I found out I was pregnant with our child, I thought it would stop.

CHAPTER 8

There was No escape

Somewhere in my already messed up mind, I had thought he would stop! Six months it lasted! Six months of not hitting me and he had also cut down on his drinking. He still didn't work. We were living in a small little flat and had met some lovely neighbours, that lived above us, and I was beginning to truly believe that the worse was over. Until he had taken the money for Jake's Easter present's and bought himself some drinks. He saw how upset I was and knew that I had done so well with paying our rent, having enough food and every day supplies.

I couldn't understand, I was standing in front of him as he was sitting on the lounge and he punched me in the stomach. I ran to the bathroom and locked the door. Tears pouring from my eyes and my body shaking. I heard him punching the walls and doors. He had always had an obsession with the movie Once were warriors and called himself Jake the Snake. I knew what he was capable of and I began to recognise, when he would snap, the warning signs. I couldn't leave as some part of me kept saying, "He is the only one who will have you. No one else would want you", and I was pregnant with his child. I noticed with my second pregnancy, that I was in pain, a constant pain, under my ribs and a ultrasound confirmed that I had a rare tumour in my liver, that would grow and stretch my liver capsules and cause me great pain.

Because of this, my second son Cameron came into the world and he was amazing. Jake loved him and and was so excited to meet him!

He looked up at me and I just knew he was special. We were living with Blakes's parents at the time, when I was in hospital; we had become friends, with the mum and dad, in the same room as what we were.

They were first time parents and in no time we became really good friends and began to visit each other. One night, Steph and doug were over at our place and were having a few drinks. I wasn't interested in drinking; I was so tired that night that I went to bed. Even with having my beautiful sons' I was unhappy and lost. The next morning, Steph had called me eager to tell me something. I really expected it to be good, but when she informed me that later that night, Blake divulged to them with glee, that Cameron was not an accident. He then had told them, that he had been placing holes in the condoms. I really could not comprehend what she was saying to me. How could this be?

It didn't take me long to confront him about it, because maybe he was just being silly, but he laughed it off with such and evil laugh, as if it was a big joke. As he said to me he didn't care he wanted his own child. I felt so sick to the stomach, what had I really gotten myself into? It would be only a few short weeks later, I would become aware, exactly what.

I had found that Doug and Steph did not actually live, where they were staying. They lived at least six hours away, They had asked us, to come up for a holiday and it was agreed as Blake wanted to get away from his patronising, mother. I was under the assumption that we were going to stay in their house. But when we actually got to the property, I found out different, they had lived in a shed down the back. It was built like a little flat, and they had put mattresses on the floor for us to stay on I was so tired. Cameron was a completely different baby to what Jake had been. I was the one that did everything.

They all wanted to stay up talking and drinking, Cameron was in his little pram, Jake on the mattress next to me. I fell asleep instantly as I could not keep my eyes open. I woke in the morning to Cameron screaming, but it wasn't his normal scream. I took him out of his pram for his early morning feed but he threw the whole lot back up. He was very unsettled and unhappy. I noticed his arm, seemed floppy.

I laid there with him, on my chest and held him, until everyone woke up. It took him a long time to settle. I expressed my concern and made an appointment with the doctor in town. I showed the doctor Cameron's arm,

Blake wasn't in there with me as he was in the waiting room with Jake. For some reason, the doctor said to me Cameron's arm was out of place and he would have to put it back into place. What was he talking about? How could my babies arm be dislocated? He must have been mistaken, all I did was go to sleep how could this have happened?

I must have done something wrong, how could I have gotten it so wrong? I couldn't stand what the doctor did next to my baby boy. I heard such a horrible noise and my beautiful boy screamed. The doctor assured me that everything was fine, Cameron's arm would be floppy for a little while longer, but it was fixed. It wasn't fine; my baby boy was throwing up everything he ate. He was beyond unhappy, so I decided to take him to the little hospital overnight. They told he had reflux, but call it mother's intuition, I knew something was wrong with my baby boy, something I couldn't explain. I was frustrated and discharged myself. Sharon may have not approved of me, but she loved her grandkids. So I rang her and asked her to come and get me.

She drove all the way up, picked us up and took myself and Cameron to the local big hospital, while Jake stayed with Blake. After a few days with tests done, yet again the doctors told me he had reflux and to thicken his milk. While he was there, they did many tests on him, including a bone test. I was relieved the day, I was given the all clear. I must have been wrong. Afterall I had taken him to a big hospital and they knew what they were doing. I had rung Sharon and told her to meet me at the front of the hospital and when I got into the car, my phone rang. At that point my life became a blur.

I completely lost sense, because I wasn't sure how I survived the call, and the following five months. The phone call was from the hospital and I was asked to bring Cameron straight back in as they had found something wrong with his bones. I went straight back up into the hospital, in the elevator my mind was going through all different scenarios, I was hoping my baby boy was okay. When the elevator door opened, standing there, were two nurses, a doctor, and a Department of Child safety case worker. I was stunned, what the hell was happening?

When I got out of the elevator, they told me I was not to leave the hospital with Cameron, why, what was going on? They then proceeded to tell me, my baby boy had three broken ribs and a broken arm. He was only six weeks old. I was told I was under investigation and I was more than welcome to go home. But Cameron had to stay until he was placed into care. What the hell were they talking about? Even with all my messed up stuff, I would never hurt my children. How did my son have broken ribs? I tried to tell them about his arm, and the doctor, but my words fell on deaf ears. While I was trying to explain to them, what I had just been through with him, in my mind I was going back over the last six weeks.

Had I done something? I looked after him, I cared for him, I loved my little man so much. How could they say what they were saying? I was told, that the injuries were related too, shaking baby syndrome. How could it be shaking baby syndrome? I had never shaken my little man. I refused to leave, I was staying there with my son. I was not allowed to do anything with my son without anyone being there observing me, I was not even allowed to draw my curtain's closed. I felt the judgement.

I wasn't the best Mom, but I tried. I had contacted Blake, in a flurry of confusion. I just could not at all, Not even for a split second, comprehend what was happening. I would not leave his side, for the fear they would take him away. A day later, I needed to go outside for a smoke and Blake had just come down. I was walking up the pathway, In such a mess. I could not stop crying as my heart had been ripped out.

I was telling him they would take our baby, angry and so weak. He stopped for a minute, on the path and turned and looked at me and had said, could it have been when you went to sleep that night, when I had, had a few drinks that I tripped on your arm and fell on him? What the hell was he trying to tell me? What had he done? I was too inconsolable to care what he was saying. I begged him, to just please tell them and make them understand it was an accident, but they said they had proof, that a babies bones were too resilient for that to be the case. So within a week, they came and took my baby away.

Five months my son was in foster care. I refused to be anywhere but where he was. So we got a horrible little flat,. A town you would miss in the blink of an eye. During those five months that my son was in care, I had, had two child safety officers resign from my case. One in tears, because she knew what they were doing was wrong. They knew I loved my children. I fought tooth and nail, every family meeting, always my question, if I was a bad mother then why did they not take Jake?

Cameron's foster mum was beautiful. It was hard for me to watch her do everything with him. An hour visit every time, but she wanted Cameron to return home to me as much as I did. She knew I did not hurt my son. Not even the police investigation went anywhere. I tried hard to prove that Cameron could come home and be safe. But they knew all to well, that it was the domestic violence. It was well known, and I was told constantly, I was a protective factor and Blake the risk factor. Fate must have stepped in for me, because of all Blake's past dealings with breaking the law, he suddenly faced going to jail.

I did not know this, but when the time came, it would literally be a blessing in disguise, one night in the flat in, as always, Blake had been drinking. It just didn't seem to me that he cared, that I was the one that wanted our son back that I was the one who would fight for him and do anything to have him returned to me. Cameron was gone, and I wasn't sure if I wasn't ever going to get him back. Because they had been talking about him becoming a ward of the state.

Blake was always a completely different person around the case Workers, and I would go along with his façade. Anything to have My Cameron returned. With all of this going on, I tried to be a good mum for my Jake. I tried to be there for him, but my heart ached for Cameron. Jake couldn't understand what was happening and how could he? His brother was there one minute then was taken the next. The night that everything escalated out of my control, I did not know, that it would change everything. I couldn't stand Blake's drinking anymore as he would leave for hours on end. He didn't care about our son.

He didn't care what he put us through; I would be waiting up till three am most mornings, not sure if I should pretend to be asleep, or appear to be awake, but no matter what, I was wronged by him. Either emotional or physical, There were times I would escape it. Those times would be, when I would get up in the morning as the sun was coming up. I would find him asleep soiled in his own excrements. This fateful night, I absolutely voiced my hate for what he had done.

It was him, he hurt our baby boy, it was because of him, I had lost Cameron. What was already a screaming match, turned quickly to blood spatter. I happened to be standing in the kitchen, the flat was strange, because our bedroom was just behind our kitchen. I was standing in front of the window yelling at him. I didn't care that this time his eyes were full of rage, but with a split second he had smashed his fist through the glass window. I was so close, that I received a blow to the nose. There was blood everywhere, I thought it was only from nose, but it was also pouring from my face. The glass had shattered and hit my face.

I didn't have enough time for the shock to wear off as I had run towards Jake. I had learned to do this often because in times like these; he would get my Jake and would not let me near him. Many times he threatened to do awful things. I knew he wasn't all there in the mind and that's what scared me. This time he wasn't going for Jake he was so enraged that he laid into me with blow after blow, punch after punch, kick after kick and knee to my head. I screamed at him "I AM SORRY!"

I tried to get his attention that there was blood everywhere and at that point I heard the heavenly sounds of sirens. Thankfully the police took him away this time. After the ambulance had left and patched me up, I collapsed on the floor. I couldn't give up now, I couldn't end it all now. I had two beautiful boys I had to protect and look after, my innocent Jake and Cameron. I couldn't take my life.

Curled up on the floor, blood everywhere, I was so tired and so worn out. I knew when the department heard about this, I would lose my Cameron forever. It wasn't my heart that ached, It was a pain that pierced my soul. Everyone I loved, had trusted even if for just a little bit, had hurt me to the core. I woke in the early hours in the morning, and the sudden realisation that I had no one, not Doug nor Steph, as they had left when I had lost my Cameron. What was wrong with me? I couldn't leave because of being fearful of loneliness. I had always seen families together and I had longed for that. How many times did I have to hear that he was sorry? How many times would I have to forgive him? How many times would I blame the alcohol and tell myself that he wasn't really like that? But he was every bit of that and more. But who else would want me? I was damaged and irreparable, I had made my bed now and I had to lie in it.

My life got so much brighter when three weeks later, Blake was sentenced to jail, for all he had done, not only to me, but his driving history. I did not see it as good to start with as now I was alone in a town, with no friends, and not a single family member, to speak of. But late one night, within a week of Blake going to jail, there was a knock at my door; it was from my case worker that I had at that time. It was around eleven thirty pm. I was frazzled with what they wanted now. I noticed instantly she wasn't dressed like a case worker, and she whispered quietly to me to come downstairs.

I had no idea what was going on! She had come on her on merit and good will, and explained to me that she could not stand what she was seeing happen to me any longer just like the last case worker that had resigned, and was refusing to stand for it any longer. She told me I was a beautiful person and a loving mom and I didn't deserve what was happening. That was only the beginning of it though. She explained that she wasn't supposed to be there, but had some very powerful advice to give.

It was explained to me that the department had said, if I had moved out of town back to where there was family support, because the risk factor had now become obsolete, and was imprisoned, that they would allow Cameron to come home. When she explained this though, she had told me in confidence, because no way, was the department going to let me know this.

The next week I packed all mine, Jake's and Cameron's stuff, I rang Kevin and Sharon and I told them I was moving back, to get my own place. I found one that was the most beautiful little home and within only a week, of settling in, Cameron's foster parents, made the trip to bring him back home to me. Five months he was gone from me and after only two weeks of his father being in prison, he was returned to me.

I was still with Blake, and on weekends I would visit with him, but on the week days, it was just Jake, Cameron and I. Jake had started day care and loved it. It also gave me the time to, spend with my little baby boy Cameron. My rent was paid and I was even able to buy special things for the boys and I, We would see Kevin and Sharon on weekends when we would all go visit Blake in prison, together. I did not like taking my children with me, but he seemed a different person, somehow, so I started thinking that prison had woken him up and made him change.

Four months I was living blissfully, I started losing a lot of weight from walking and just being happy. We never went without and I began to take pride in myself again. Something I hadn't done for such a long time. It didn't last. He came home and had the department come into my life again.

A case Worker came around and explained to me that, Cameron should never have come home and if it was her, she would take him back off me. I had to do an intensive care program and for a while, things were good and it seemed like we were a good little family. But he would want to go over to his parents a lot and start taking over the finances. So the rent began to, once again, fall behind and if he didn't work nor get a job, then I would. So I did! I gained employment at a factory and even though I didn't have a license, or car I found my way to and from work.

I loved it and I would make sure Blake and my boys, were at his parent's house. I was still doing everything with the boy's and going to work, until I received a phone call early one morning. I was sitting at the train station, almost falling asleep, from the ten hours of night shift from the previous night, which I had just completed.

I would normally come home and feed the boys breakfast, make sure everything was okay, have a shower then try and get a few hours' sleep, before I had to get up and do it all again. The call was from Blake, telling me that I my legal representation had called, and he had great news for me. When I was eighteen, I was contacted by a government organization, which had informed me, I was entitled to compensation, for the sexual abuse. I really didn't care at the time, No amount of money, could take away the pain, which was inside of me every day.

Three days later I was in a meeting with my lovely solicitor, he handed me a cheque, for thousands of dollars! I had been to a hearing six months earlier, as the judge stated if he could give me more, he would, because of the results of my psychological reports that I had been made to take. I knew that is was not going to be good because, I couldn't pretend. It basically said, that I wasn't coping with life, and hadn't done for a long time I had never seen so much money.

The moment it was in my bank, I wanted it gone. I began to feel very angry inside, and yet again, I began my steep and fast decline. I had allowed my old friend Natasha, to come back, into my life and in doing so, I allowed her to steal, a lot of money from me, after I had given her some to help her in her current situation. I even let her partner inject speed, into my arm. My life was out of control, I couldn't stop what was happening. I was beyond any help.

Everything that I had bought out of the money, that wasn't stolen, was eventually hocked into the pawn shop, even the car that I had purchased. What had happened to my life? It was so wonderful, when it was just Jake, Cameron and I, and just like many times before, we were evicted. Why was I letting this happen to me? Why couldn't I just run away, with my boys? The night that the speed was injected into my own arm, I knew that I could never do it again. The feeling of absolute bliss, I was on cloud nine, no worries in the world at all.

It was not long, that I began to see Natasha for what she really was, And told her to get out of my life and never come back. If taking thousands of dollars from me wasn't enough, I caught her stealing a measly $20 from my purse. I had lost absolutely everything in four short weeks. Left with nowhere to go again, I refused to live with Kevin and Sharon, and my boys needed a home. There was a fear inside of me, that Blake's family were trying to take Jake and Cameron I wasn't aware, and was in complete shock, when I found out I was pregnant for a third time.

I couldn't do it. Not again. Another child for me to screw up, I was sinking deeper and deeper into the pit of darkness. Eventually the thoughts I had fought all of my life, began to resurface and again I wanted to die. My children would be better off without me; I couldn't let it happen, so I kept fighting myself for my children. Through some form of miracle, my brother's and father had gotten in contact with me. They were living in their own place. I was so happy and relieved to hear that he had left Carol.

Things were okay again, I was with my brothers and father and Blake would never dare to hurt me with my brothers and father around, I was safe. My brothers had started talking to me and telling me they were being used by my father because of their disabilities. All of the bills were in their names, as they both had jobs and he was taking all of their money. It was very sad when I started seeing it myself. He cared only for himself. My brothers were literally his meal ticket. So taken a role I had played years ago, I told the boys to come with me. Even the house was in Corey's name. I had a confrontation with my father about what was happening.

With such coldness, he kicked us all out. We were all completely homeless, a couple of nights in hotels here and there, until I eventually found a caravan. I thought making contact with my mum, would help, by asking her if she would take the boys back and look after them. But of course she refused. They wanted to control my life, not theirs. I had to look after my brothers and make sure they were okay, while still making sure, Blake had money for his alcohol, anything to make sure I was okay.

I was heavily pregnant, there was four adults and two children living in a caravan, for weeks I rung around all the welfare agencies, to try and find us a home. I was put on waiting list upon waiting list upon waiting list. There was not enough money to support us, no jobs. Blake had, had two jobs the whole time I had been with him that had lasted only a week or two. One late night in the caravan, when my two brothers and Blake were having a drink.

I heard Blake talking about an armed robbery. Honestly I didn't think any of it, because many times he had declared he would go rob something but he never did. I wasn't coherent enough to take notice, even when they went to the shop the next day and bought toy guns and painted them black. I was suspended in my thoughts and my own fantasies, an absolute lost cause. Sitting for hours with a blank look on my face, not noticing what was going on around me, in pain. But it wasn't just the pain from my soul; I was physically in pain from my third pregnancy.

Maybe they had told me what they had planned but I had not acknowledged it. I would be spoken to and not even realise, somewhere else was better where I was. Either way I was just as bad as them. Not even, the night that they bought money home from somewhere. I had believed they had gotten cash in hand jobs. I was sort of talking to my mother at this stage. Driving around in a car without a license. I didn't know what I wanted anymore. I had turned the auto pilot mode on, living the best way possible. All the while such a feeling of emptiness inside of me grew. Everyone telling to have faith and that GOD would take care of me. What Frigging GOD? There was no GOD.

One morning, I was out driving with my little sister Sarah, trying to mend any bit of the relationship that we had. I was pulled over by the police, told the car was unregistered and given fines, the police officer was nice enough to drop Sarah off at Mum's and me all the way to the caravan we were staying in at a deserted show grounds. I was scared to even get out of the police car, knowing I had not bought the car back. I didn't really have time to think about anything let alone do anything, because as the police car left, my mum's car appeared, with my mum, brothers, step dad and sisters all in it.

All of a sudden Blake and Corey were hiding. If my step dad had known Blake was there he wouldn't have been able to control himself. I was sitting there astounded, because Corey and Shaun had actually come out and for the first time in nine years the whole family was all together. It was like nothing had ever happened. I had completely forgotten about Blake hiding, until my younger sister had whispered to my mum that she had been in the caravan and had seen Blake.

That was all it took. My step dad barged in and within two minutes outran Blake four government cars drove into the show grounds and if that wasn't enough suddenly there was police everywhere. What was happening? No one was telling me anything; I was beyond shock especially when they took all my brothers And Blake away. Still no answers, no one would tell me anything, with my hand on my belly and my eyes on my little men, I knew I had to prepare myself. because honestly all I had ever experienced was the bad.

After hours of sitting in the police station, not being given any answers, the penny finally dropped. I was taken outside by a lovely detective and informed, that Corey, Shaun and Blake had committed four armed robberies and it was because I was pulled up that day, in the getaway car, that they were able to find them. I felt sick, so sick to my stomach. They were all going to go to jail, it was because of me. I was disgusted in myself. Hating myself, For taking my brothers away from the home, they lived in before I came into their lives again.

Blake was so, lucky, that the detective had such a kind heart and took into account my pregnancy and the situation that we were in. So he had explained to us that Blake would be given a special order allowed to stay out of prison, until the sentencing, which would give him plenty of time, to be there when our new baby was born. He had to behave and do the right thing, because yet again, I found us living with his parents. Our baby girl was born six weeks early because of the tumour in my liver. I had to go and be induced. I was not in a good space, physically mentally or emotionally. It was the most traumatic labour I ever had.

Twenty four hours I was in labour with my little girl, only being four centre metres dilated, the epidural had paralysed me and I could not feel my legs from my hips down. I could see that and the nurses were becoming constantly worried, I was throwing up from the gas. Everything was becoming a blur to me. I recall the doctor being called in, because both my baby and I were under so much stress. I was so weak. I just wanted to sleep. I remember the nurse attaching a drip to me and pressing so many times on the little button and asking me how I felt? I instantly felt so tired. All I could do was go to sleep.

That's what I thought I was doing, until I found myself back in that calm place, everything so quiet. I was watching myself appear to be sleeping; I saw Blake leave the room as he told the nurses he was going for a smoke. Then loud noises bells going off everywhere and at least six people rushed into the room. A mask was put on my face and my gown was ripped open. Then I found myself in my body again. I opened my eyes to a bright light; I felt the oxygen mask on my face. And the caring doctor looked down at me and stated to me welcome back.

The rest of my labour was such a blur, I do recall my legs being put in stirrups and the nurse explaining to me, my baby girl had to go into a special care nursery as soon as she was born because of what had happened. I wasn't really aware of when my baby girl came into the world. I could not feel my legs for hours after her birth. I do remember trying to sit up, when I could feel my legs a little bit. I tried to stand up, I just wanted to have a shower, but I fell straight to the floor.

Eventually when the doctors gave me the all clear, I was wheeled out of the delivery room in a wheelchair, but as I passed the midwives desk, she smiled at me, and said that it was nice to see me as she thought I had left them for good. All I wanted to do was see my baby girl Amber, because she was so perfect, and it was because of that, having not a single thing wrong with her, she was able to stay with me in my room.

When I showered and recovered that night, I laid in bed holding my baby girl so tight. I could not let her go, not for one second, so she slept in bed with me. The next morning, being less in a daze, two men in black suits walked into my room, they asked me to sign papers. I couldn't understand what they were trying to tell me or what they were trying to say. They had asked if I had any intention of seeking legal advice. What were they talking about my baby girl was alive wasn't she?

I signed their papers, and didn't take any notice of them. Not them, nor the anaesthesiologist, that had come to see me, and explain, they put it down to a reaction to the drug. I knew what I had seen though, that nurse pressing so many times on that pain relief, I was just so relieved that my baby girl and I were here together. Even the hospital social worker came to see me as he had heard what had happened. I repeatedly told him everything was okay and I was fine, because I honestly did think it was.

Even living at Kevin and Sharon's I was just so grateful to be back, but that was until the homecare nurse came around to visit a few days later. She was only there for a routine visit, but it was in black and white on her paper, that I had died. Everything was such a blur then, I just wanted to get away. Get away from Blake, get away from everything. I took the action steps and I got us a home. Cameron and Jake loved their little baby sister, she truly was a miracle. I had such beautiful children.

The couple of months that Blake had without going to prison, he completely destroyed, with only weeks within leaving his parents. He got in a car and drove, but not only was he caught once; he was caught three times in the same night. So when I found out, when the police bought Jake home that night. The next day I travelled by bus and train to the courthouse, to wait eight hours, with my one month old baby girl. The boys were safely being looked after, the judge had seen me there all day and even came over to admire Amber, when I walked into the courtroom at four pm she put her head down, and then looked over at me. The Judge apologised to me and then spoke to Blake.

She explained to him, having such a precious new born baby and loyal partner didn't stop him from reoffending so he would be put on remand until his sentencing. That was it. I had absolutely had too much this time. On the bus home that afternoon, my heart heavy, I was over all this shit, over the life I was living, but I didn't have the guts to leave him. I only stayed in that house for a couple of months. It didn't matter how many times the neighbour had warned be about the landlord, I did not believe it because she had given us a home.

Unexpectedly, I became good friends with a young mum two houses down. Even more unexpectedly, my Brother Wayne was dating her. Kevin and Sharon had started babysitting the children every second weekend and it was on those times; I drank and smoked so much pot that I could not function. I felt that Wayne and I were getting close, because he and Anna would come and spend so much time with me. My brother hadn't witnessed me at my worst.

We had begun talking, deeper than I ever thought I could talk to my brother. It had to be when I was heavily intoxicated though, I began to trust him enough, when I opened up, and told him about what our next door neighbour had done. I did not have to say much, because he knew. In that split second I shut down, what did he mean he knew? How dare he? If he knew why didn't he try and stop it or tell someone? He tried to explain to me why, but I was a mess. My brother knew exactly how much pain I suffered, that night when I told him I just wanted to die. He held my hair as I threw up, put me in the shower with my clothes on and looked after me. Unfortunately that would be the last time I would open up to anyone. It was truly confirmed for me, I could not put my trust in anyone.

When Wayne took my friend Anna home to meet our parents, just as always, I was rejected. He was made to choose either myself or them and it was always them. Once again a pain in my heart so strong? Where else did I have to go, but straight back to Blake, when he was released months later. I could not care anymore; I just wanted to run far away from everything. It suited me when we ended up in a little town, with only four houses and a pub in the middle of nowhere. I didn't want to be near anyone, let alone meet anyone.

I had now come to terms with the fact that I was worthless and nothing good would come my way. Eventually, the next door neighbour Katie came over and introduced herself to us. She had two daughters and was completely different to anyone I had ever before met. We began to spend a lot of time together as there was nothing else to do. I tried to force myself to be a friend; it was very hard keeping up with her and Who she liked and disliked. One day she would be talking to someone and the next she wasn't. I found if I just agreed with her, everything would be okay.

I also began to notice, the tension between katie and Blake, she liked him and he was constantly flirting with her. So when he would leave the children and I at home to go next door, I was secretly wishing that they were sleeping together, I don't know if they ever did as he would never admit it. But yet again, living there did not last long, because again he had been caught driving without a license and instead of giving his brother's name like he had done times before; he lied and gave the officer a fake name.

He tried to get away with it, by having tattoos of the children's names put on his neck, but really the police were not stupid, and yet again he was back in court. And once again, we were back at his parents. I am not sure how it happened, but he had run into Natasha one day and assured me, that she had changed. She had her own place, was doing well for herself and had two children.

Again, I was playing with fire, walking where angels dare not tread. We were living with Natasha at this stage and I thought everything was going okay. Having her children and being what she had been through I honestly thought she was past all her crap. But it wasn't so. After a night of drinking, I ended up in Natasha's bed. I just wanted a home, a home with my children. That white picket fence dream, constantly every day of my life, fighting the need to die, knowing my children would probably be better off without me, hoping the right people would show up, who I could know would love them, care for them and give them everything they needed. Everything that I could not, because for such a long time now, I knew that I could not love my children.

If this was love, then I didn't want it, ever, because to me, love equalled pain and suffering and trust equalled only loss and loneliness. Eventually I fell off to sleep, but awoke to the bed moving and moaning noises. I knew exactly what those noises were, right beside me, Blake and Natasha were doing the unthinkable. Did they think I was stupid? They said that they wanted a threesome and they were just starting without me. I was so enraged. I put my children in the car and screaming at them. After everything they had both put me through how dare they?

Natasha was threatening to ring the police, and was begging me to go back inside and to just get over it. Who was I kidding I had nowhere to go? So I walked back inside, fear was gripping me, leaving me paralysed, how could this be my life? I found myself back in that courthouse a few weeks later when yet again, Blake was sent to jail. Things had become very frosty between Natasha and I. I tried to stay out of that house as much as I could. Every day searching for somewhere else to live, the hate I felt towards her growing. Even the fact, that I had wiped her when she had stolen thousands of dollars from me, the moment she walked into my life, she had caused me trouble, I could feel that something would happen. and It was only the next day; it ended in a physical altercation. I hadn't been in a fight with anyone since I had been a teenager. I felt I could have killed her that day but I had to stop myself.

All the things I owned were sitting in her garage. Something had to give, something had to happen for me, and it did. To my great relief, an older friend whom I had met, that had lived across the road from Katie's and I had rung me with the news, he had found somewhere for us to go. He even made the three hour drive down with a trailer and picked all of my stuff up, took the kids and I back, to his friend's house and that's when I met Robert and Tarni.

They were so lovely and said we could stay as long as we needed, it was at this time, that I made my first name change, I had been to hell and back, had my fair share of pain, dragged my children along for the ride, I did not belong anywhere, so why shouldn't I change my name? I thought if I changed my name that I would be a new person.

CHAPTER 9

Courage Found

I found myself, visiting Blake, out of pity, because it wasn't the same. I had become stronger; I was determined to take all of my power back. The first step, I took, was I refused to take my children into that horrible place anymore. I was in contact with my younger brother Corey. He had done nine months in jail for the armed robbery, but no longer talked to my brother Shaun. There was a nasty rift, as Shaun did not go to jail yet he and Blake had. I was able to visit Corey twice when he was in jail and then when he got out and informed me he was expecting a child, I was so happy for him. I was finding the courage and the strength, to leave Blake after nearly six years and eventually I had found the most wonderful home for my children and myself.

Our first real home, because that's what it was. I had become really close to Tarni and Robert, and even their housemate Greg. So when he asked me he if he could move into my garage and help me out, I thought that was great. I didn't see him becoming very possessive and consequently ruined my friendship with Tarni and Robert.

Out of the blue, talking with Corey one night, he told me he had Katie's number, and I should ring her. I had to think about it for a while and thought maybe if I had changed she had as well. I really had nothing else to lose, so I sat on my front step and made the call. We spoke for a while and had to assure her that the rumours of me being a meth head were far from the truth. Things then moved rapidly fast.

She wanted to come and see me that night and bring her friend with her, I thought yes, that was fine as we had a lot to catch up on. And for the very first time, I was proud of myself, for what I had. But not only what I had, how far I had come.

Katie and her friend Suzy turned up. Appearance wise she hadn't changed at all, I couldn't help to notice her friend though as she was quite funny, smoking a cigar, and commenting on my house. Clearly she was intoxicated, because only an hour later, she passed out on my bed. That night, I decided that I had judged Katie to harshly, so the next couple of days were spent together, she would come over or I would visit her.

She began to tell me all about Suzy and how they met, so it didn't surprise me that we ended up at Suzy's house, she wanted to prove to me that Suzy's brother eric, who was only nineteen, had a crush on her. The way Katie spoke, every man wanted her, I sat uncomfortably in Suzy's lounge room, there was alcohol everywhere and I think Katie proved her point when Eric got up and sat right next to her while Suzy was talking to me.

It wouldn't be, for a good couple of weeks after that night, that I really got to know Suzy better. I used to help Katie clean for her sister in law, so when she asked me if I wanted to do it again, I jumped at the opportunity. My wonderful friend Mark, who had saved me and helped me, turned up one day, and literally gave me a car. I was so grateful and I loved when he would visit me, always trying to help me with something.

The day that I applied for my learners and got them, was yet another stepping stone, because for years that was one thing Blake would not let me do. He would constantly ring me, phone call after phone call. Every time I heard that jail message, I slammed down the receiver. In the past when he had been in jail, I would have to go without to send him money. So when I refused, to do it this time, I was taking more of my power back. I had to pay my rent; I wasn't going to suffer and go without and I enjoyed being able to buy my children everything. I had my own money to do with, whatever I pleased. This was new to me, all of it was.

Even better was, I was making some really good friends and even better they were really good people. It was suzy and her family, I found out very quickly that I had not judged Katie to harshly, she had not changed.

Constantly belittling people and talking bad about people. What right did she have? No one was perfect I knew that, because I was the absolute proof of that. Just as fast that Katie phased into my life, she faded back out of it. Having to see her every day and every night was too much. Before I realised this though, I was invited to a party, where I was able to get to know suzy's Brother Eric I hadn't been drinking and was completely coherent.

I had, had just about enough of the sleazy guy who kept touching me and hitting on me and would not get the hint. I was having a good night except for that. I rang Greg my housemate and asked if he would drive out and come and get me. I was supposed to stay that night, but I felt better going home. Eric and His Girlfriend felt the same, so I gave them a lift home; I was quite relieved that I was able to get to know Grant because I opened my door to him a few days later. In his arms was his baby nephew. I couldn't turn him away as he was a nice guy and he had a little baby in his arms. I took charge immediately who wouldn't?

Evan was such an adorable Baby, and my baby Amber just happened to be turning two, so I did not mind at all, it was nothing. Eric explained to me that Suzy was in hospital and he was unsure what to do. I told him to stay put and drove up to the home, and got everything that Little Evan needed. suzy's partner was an interstate truck driver. It turned out, that Suzy wasn't going to come home. I drove to the hospital let her know what was happening and reassure her that her little man was safe. She had known me long enough to know this.

Suzy was such a funny person and mum, unconventional in so many ways. It was this, which I most enjoyed about her. Being around her really was a breath of fresh air, always making me laugh and look at her with shock, as well as Suzy I was getting to know Eric a lot better. My housemate Greg was still living with me, and I was very fast noticing that he was becoming strange. He tried to get close to my children and I, but at no time, did I ever give him the impression that I would be anything other than his friend and housemate. It was this reason that I asked Eric to stay one night. Greg had gotten very possessive and angry earlier that day.

Somewhere in my mind, I thought maybe if he saw another guy there that he would back off, Eric was a nice guy, we only had a couple of drinks, but it was that night, that I was starting to realise that with all the new beginning's happening for me and all the courage I needed, had built, and I was ready, to officially leave Blake and never return. I was not alone and more than ready to let go of the old life, I had been living for so long. I took one last call from the jail the next morning, this time I was too happy, in getting myself and my life together for my children and I. It really was over, and I had to do it while he was still behind bars. It was the most courageous decision that I had made, for a very long time and actually followed through with it.

The last call that came through I wasn't scared, I actually felt strong and I finally told Blake that I was done. That we were over, and inside of me was nothing but hate for him. I really didn't care, he tried all of his old tricks on me, begged me, pleaded me, but this time his words fell on deaf ears. That was it, my phone rung constantly. I was free, I did not have to tell him that I loved him, I hung up the phone that day, and I felt like, I was a bird that was finally freed from its cage.

CHAPTER 10

The Tide Changes

I did not tell Kevin and Sharon straight away, what business was it of theirs anyway? Sharon had put the blame on me for everything. Even for Blake being in jail, the only thing that really made me sad, was I would miss talking to Kevin. He was such an amazing man. The years I spent trying to work out Kevin and his brother Ryan were everything that Blake was not, but never was my question answered. I was elated that I would never have to put up with Sharon's patronising ways or dirty looks, her constant judgement. I couldn't stand people who were nice to your face and nasty behind your back. So many years saying sorry for everything. Never having to justify myself to them again. The only thing that I could be grateful for was that my children had wonderful grandparents. Or so I thought.

Unfortunately it was nearly five years later, that the truth would be revealed in many ways. Kevin and Sharon would take the children when they could, that would mean a break for me. It wasn't easy trying to raise three children on my own. To make it that little bit more complex, Jake had just been diagnosed with ADHD and Asperger's. I had known there was something different about him but honestly I blamed myself for that, I thought the life that he lived with me, was what made him so different.

But it wasn't until his school teacher informed me, that she had worked with students for twenty years that had Asperger's, so she wrote up a large report, and from a checklist of forty, thirty eight boxes were ticked. I was relieved, I had never considered, that he had a medical condition, either way he was special to me. Even though I was only on my learners, I would still drive around. It scared me, and every time I saw a police car, I flinched. So the morning that I was supposed to take my children to visit with their grandparents, I asked eric if he would drive the children and I down as he was full licensed. I told him it would be a couple of hours trip, and he agreed. He was such a mature lovely guy for his age, and he had his own life worries.

Nine hours later we were on our way back home, Eric and I had spent the whole day broken down on the side of the road and Kevin being as wonderful as he was, did not stop, until my car was back on the road. That day was a sad day for me, because I realised I was going to miss him quite a lot. Regardless what he may have honestly thought about me, he never showed it. And always made me laugh. I had so much respect for him for that. It was cold driving home that night, my windows had stopped working. As much as I was glad to be going home, I was dreading having to put up with Greg. Maybe that's what Eric had picked up on when he asked if I wanted to go back to their place.

I honestly just wanted to go home and shower and got to bed, knowing I could sleep in, in the morning. What did I have to lose though, really? By the time we got back there, it was already late and suzy was out of hospital and my children were not there, even when I wanted and needed a break, the moment they left I was lost and I knew, every time I would plan on sleeping in, it never happened. When we eventually walked in the door that night, I was in for a bit of a shock. She had been prescribed strong pain killers and was completely dosed up and as high as a kite.

The day had been mentally draining, suzy was sitting at the table and told me instead of going home I could just bunk in eric's bed. I couldn't believe what I was hearing and I was feeling quite uncomfortable, I could have gotten in my car an driven home, but something made me stay. Eric had a girlfriend and as far as they all knew I was still with Blake. It was no one's business that I hated him and our relationship was over.

Having people know that I had a partner that was in prison was a safety net for me and protected me in my own way. Knowing this when I got into Eric's bed made it a little less uncomfortable. I made it very clear that there was a boundary line between us, with a rolled up blanket. Being nervous and very anxious, I couldn't sleep and talked for quite a while, until I fell asleep.

I awoke the next morning not knowing that is was the morning of a life changing event for me. After a day spent shopping as a twenty three year old shopping with my friends, it was arranged that I would have drinks with them that night and get to know Suzy's partner John. The neighbour also came over that night, I was thoroughly enjoying myself. Every hour that passed, we were all becoming more intoxicated. That wasn't always a good thing. I could feel the tension between Eric and John. Things were certainly heated. I knew all too well the signs, being with an alcoholic, I was able to feel and see when a fight would start.

And when someone had consumed too much alcohol, I wasn't too bothered because for once I wasn't worried about my own protection. All I heard was John telling Eric that he was the King and Eric the prince, before a fight started, that would leave John burnt from a deep fryer, screaming at Eric to go back to his home town. Suzy was a mess trying to look after her younger brother and partner. I am really not sure how it escalated how it did. All I knew was, I couldn't let that nice guy, have nowhere to go. And I wanted to help Suzy, too many times, I had no one to help me when I needed. It was the least I could do to offer Eric my couch till he was able to get things together.

Unexpectedly I found myself outside talking to John, it was one of the sick jokes of my life, I was able to talk to and somehow get through to people but I was unable to help myself. john wasn't a bad guy, I picked up from him that night, that he had not had the best childhood either. I don't think he honestly meant it to happen the way it did. They had both had, too much to drink. I had learned over the years that the ego would come out of people, when too much alcohol was consumed.

I was intoxicated, but not completely so that I was not coherent and able to snap into action, you become quite good at that when you have to do it quite regularly, Suzy had to look after he little family, the best thing I could do for her was take her brother back to my house so he was safe. Doing that, I didn't realise, that it would have such an impact on Greg, and that he would become quite nasty towards me. He had something against Eric. But I was too blind to see that it was jealousy. That night as

I lay in my big beautiful bed I couldn't help but to wonder where my life was going. I had already lived through so much suffering and unhappiness. The loneliness alway's there, it wasn't loneliness of being single though, it was the loneliness that had been present all my life.

I missed my munchkins, and wondered just how much things would change when Blake's parents found out that I had left him, and no matter what I would never be going back. I now knew that I was scared of allowing myself, to open to anyone ever again. I didn't want love. It wasn't real, it was cruel, for some reason I cried myself to sleep that night, but it wasn't a soulful cry it was a soft cry. The tears would not stop falling; it really was the end of a very dark chapter of my life.

Having Eric living there wasn't a threat as I enjoyed his company in my own way. Such a soft different personality that I had never come across and I put it down to where they had grown up, my heart would go out to him, he had his own problems and was probably as lost as what I was. he was really good with children and had such a soft spot, especially for his little nephew.

With Eric living there, Suzy would visit more often, we would have lunch and start, hanging around a lot together.I found it funny, when she would mention to me, that she had a rule, that no one was allowed to sleep with her brother. Honestly the thoughts that would go through my mind, when she said that. No one would want me; I was damaged goods even before I was in Blake's stranglehold. And I was definitely never, going to let anyone in. Apart from that, I hadn't even, considered, looking at another man.

Even with Blake's disloyalty, never once, did I do wrong by him or break the bonds of loyalty. I didn't realise, that when my brother Corey would come up and visit, that I would hit absolute rock bottom and I would change my life, even more than what I already had. When corey and his girlfriend, Amanda came to stay with me. I hadn't seen him, since I was able to visit him when he was in jail. So much had happened in both our lives; we had hours' worth of catching up to do.

Even with drinking as much as what I did, never once, would I allow my children to see me intoxicated as they were always in bed. Jake and Cameron had already witnessed enough traumas in their short lives. I absolutely loved having my brother up with me, showing him how far I had actually come. But I barely tolerated Amanda, his girlfriend, because my brother was unaware, of the way she would look at Eric with puppy dog eyes. It was obvious to me that Corey and Amanda were not as involved with each other as they made out.

I could not blame my brother because When he went to jail, Amanda had slept with someone else and had gotten herself pregnant. But I snapped out of it, because I really couldn't judge anyone after the life that I had lived. Eric and Corey got a long great; it seemed that everyone at my place suited each other. With the exception of Greg.

One of the nights we were all outside drinking with all of my children safe sleeping in bed, I finally spoke the words to someone, it was corey, my brother, I told him that I had left Blake and promised him that I was never going back. It felt so good, like a huge weight had been lifted off of me. No longer, did I have to pretend that I was still in a relationship; I was now safe and free. I tried to explain to him and even tried to justify why I stayed, why I put myself and my innocent children through six traumatic years of darkness. My brother then proceeded to confirm, what I had thought was a rumour, about an incident, that had occurred three years earlier. Corey had heard, that Blake had taken, money off, the perverted older man who was obsessed with me.

He told me, that the older man had told Corey, that Blake let him put a drug in my drink, take me upstairs from where we staying and take advantage of me. My heart went straight into my stomach. I felt violently ill. Blake had sat in that court room the day of my compensation hearing and had heard everything that had happened to me. I couldn't think straight, every rape that my body had endured, came rushing back to me. I couldn't stay there, I couldn't cope with this anymore, I managed to lift myself out of the chair, I couldn't say much except I was going for a walk.

I wasn't angry I was enraged. The tears would not stop falling from my eyes; I relived all of the horrible, nasty, evil things that, that man had put me through. The hatred I had for myself, for staying for so long. I couldn't understand why I stayed. Was loneliness truly much worse than what I had endured? I was struggling, my reality was slipping away. Walking down the road I hadn't realised that Eric was following me he had become a friend. But I did not want anyone near me, I had spent so many years in this head space. Knowing it wasn't healthy, but also knowing, I would never be destined for happiness. I was damaged, torn up, rejected. I hadn't been happy, I had just been putting a mental block over what was really happening.

I was in the midst, of the darkness again.

I kept telling Eric I was fine and wanted to be alone, how could he, even begin to understand what was going on inside of me? But he refused to leave my side and sat and listened to my self pity for hours. We were sitting so close together, I don't know how it happened, but that night was the beginning, of a sexual relationship.

It was strange for me but I made it very clear that it was just sex. The truth was, he was the first man that I had ever slept with that gave me pleasure. I did not feel scared or angry nor feel the need to push him off me. Maybe this was why; I couldn't keep my hands off him?

For two weeks straight I was intoxicated day and night, bottle after bottle, because if I stopped drinking, I would have to feel again. What had I done to deserve anything of which was forced upon me? The question I asked myself my through my whole life, how could there be a GOD. No GOD would make me live, through what I have lived through. Even with all of this going on inside of me, I couldn't stop myself from sleeping with Eric. And he had begun sleeping in my bed. There was a still boundary though; I would make sure there was no cuddling or kissing.

For me it was the best sex I had ever had. He couldn't understand why I never opened my eyes while we were having sex, but he did not realise I couldn't let anyone look into my eyes. I noticed emotions coming up, and then one night, he put his blanket over me and held me. I was realising that it was more than just sex; I really didn't want this happening. I kept telling myself I was not falling for him.

He was five years younger, Suzy's brother and I had three children, and how could I allow this to happen? I didn't want any of this, and I knew that nothing good had lasted in my life, nothing good at all. I had all of the excuses to stop myself from falling, but my heart was doing something different. His clothes started appearing in my cupboard. I took them out and put them on the floor. There had to be a boundary. Things were moving so fast, had I not learnt my lesson with love, already.

My brother corey was there with me for weeks, witnessing my decline, helping me look after my children while I was in an alcohol induced daze, not only that again I had started smoking pot. I was honestly trying to catch up, did I miss something? I was having trouble comprehending anything. Maybe I pushed him away, but just like the others my brother turned on me. It didn't surprise me. It was funny though because the day after he left, I awoke early while it was still dark, after weeks of fuzziness, I just accepted what was happening and let myself cry.

That morning I stopped all of the drinking and the head space disappeared. I didn't know it at the time, but I had tapped into an amazing power. Eric had just expressed being in love with me, three months we had lived together as friends, not once did I think I was going to fall in love. As expected I had done wrong by my friend Suzy and she was not happy as I had broken her rule. But she had to understand I never saw it coming. I never expected to fall in love with her brother. There were still trials for me as Blake was about to be released, and even though I had admitted I loved Eric to myself I still had insecurities that he would hurt me.

Greg had finally gotten the hint and realised it was time for him to leave. I had heard people talking about the honeymoon period all of my life and how blissful it was, but never had I had the opportunity to experience for myself. But now I was living it. I swear the love I felt for this man, I had never felt for anyone. It was not just me that adored him, my children did as well, especially my little Amber. It was very conflicting for me as it was quite clear to me I was falling in love but it scared me. There was a fear there and it would grip me, maybe he would get sick of me? Or even hurt me? But he was so soft, my life then changed even more than I could have imagined.

I had just turned twenty four years old, I was sitting on my lounge one night and Eric came in, knelt down in front of me and told me he was moving back home, that he loved me and wanted me to go with him. I was in shock, I didn't even know where his home towm was. I had never been out of the state. After thinking about it and admitting it not only to myself, but finally letting the words come out and tell him that I loved him and it was real. I made the choice to move and follow my heart.

Blake was a week from being released, the thought of being that far away from him in another state made me feel safer than I had felt in years. It hit me subtlety that this really was the ending and new beginning for me. I was extremely excited for my children, Suzy and John were moving back as well. With everything put behind us, all forgiven, She became my best friend and it didn't take long for everything to happen. Kevin and Sharon now knew that Blake and I were separated and I was with someone else. They could think what they wanted really, after the life I had lived with their son.

The children were down visiting their Grandparents and their father for the first time. That was the day that Suzy, John, Eric myself and Evan, took a road trip to meet Eric's family for the first time. We were also down there to look at the local rental properties. Eric and I applied for the bigger one. I took a great leap of faith when weeks later, I packed up and prepared to move interstate. It was an eye opener for me.

All anyone seemed to do was drink and smoke weed. It wasn't an easy time for me as moving I had to let my Jake go, due to his ADHD and Asperger's I wasn't able to support him in the ways he needed and his grandparents would be able to give him everything he needed. We lived in there for twelve months and the honeymoon period was over. I had started to push Eric away, not understanding what I was doing. I missed my son so much that my heart ached.

I had lost Jake to that family years earlier. I didn't realise, that the Lawson family would have an unhealthy hold over me for years to come. When Blake wasn't trying everything in his power to sweet talk me to get me back he was showing me his true self. I could literally feel the anger hatred and disgust simmer, knowing that he was good at making himself, out to be better than what he truly was. In time, I would stop dealing with him and go through his parents. He tried to turn Jake against me, so many horrible things that were said to me, if I asked for the children to go up for the weekend or the holidays he would constantly put me down and belittle me. Even when he got a girlfriend, I would receive obscene messages, if I wasn't with him, he was going to make my life a misery as much as he could.

That meant interfering and manipulating my relationship with Eric. I was too blind to see, that I was still in his hold. If I had even known what

I found out years later, I would have stopped all contact with the man. He wasn't a man, he was a monster he preyed on the weak, every phone call I had from him it would spark such a fury within me that would show up In my relationship with Eric, Consequently we began to fight constantly.

When it was good, it truly was wonderful, never would he be physically, or intentionally hurt me. Because of my insecurities within myself, he then began to go out drinking. I didn't realise that subconsciously I was waiting for him to become like Blake. I knew in the core of my being that it was never love with Blake nor Luke and it was knowing that, that I began to feel really frustrated at wanting to leave Eric. I wasn't scared of being alone, but I didn't believe that Eric loved me.

To me it seemed that just the sex was keeping us together. I tried to love him as much as I could, as much as I could love anyone, even my own children, but my heart was tarnished. I couldn't express it. How could I express it, when I didn't know what it was or why it was happening? I found it very difficult to look people in the eyes; maybe it was my lack of self-worth or that if they looked into my eyes they could see my soul.

Eric's twin, brother, Peter was a bachelor. He worked at the same farm where Eric worked. They looked nothing alike and were different in so many ways, but yet the same in other. Our time spent in there, was having people over for drinks, socialising, Pete and Suzy would spend a lot of time with us. We went camping together, every week Suzy and I would go to the nearest shops thirty minutes away. I tried to be happy, I knew I had no reason not to be happy, but it didn't work. I may have had a smile on my face, but I was struggling inside.

Why would it not just go away? This horrible sensation in my being, I wanted to be happy, feel alive, I just didn't know how to be. What was it that other people had that I lacked? What made everyone else happy and not me? I would sit and watch people for hours, trying to see if they had something I did not. Eric would have to drive everywhere because I only had my learners. It was a lot to ask of him, he always made the trip up so my children could visit, with their Grandparents and their father. He did not agree with it, but still did it for me.

We split up a few times, but within a few days were back together again, the amount of times I tried to fit in, I seemed to cause more trouble or heart ache for myself. I had, had enough of where we lived, I had enough of sitting around and doing nothing, but even more so I wanted my Jake home, for this to happen I needed to move away, So we moved to the beautiful coast. Suzy and John had also moved too. And Jake thankfully was home with us again.

Eric was looking for work, as we were about to get a big shock, I was pregnant.

We moved around quite a lot trying to get a good job for Eric and unfortunately we ended straight back up where we had moved from, when I was twenty eight weeks pregnant. Just like my last pregnancies there were complications, but this time, I would be in hospital, seven weeks before our baby was born, nine weeks early. The tumour in my liver had grown very large. I was in agonising pain.

For six weeks I was given high doses of morphine and methadone, from a PCA machine. Every time I pressed the button it would administer pain relief. It was hard for me to hear I was given methadone, it really angered me. Wasn't that just for people recovering from addictions? But the doctor explained to me, because of the amount of morphine that was administered to me, I needed the methadone. My health was deteriorating, bedridden, not being able to eat, let alone going to the toilet on my own, I lost seventeen Kilo's, it was unbearable.

When I was initially admitted, the doctors had to contact a specialist who described my condition as it was very rare. I was being monitored every day by three different teams of doctors. The concern was that the tumour could rupture, and mine and my unborn baby's life could be in danger. I missed Eric and my children so much; they were hours away from me. I did not get to see my children for three months. Blake would ring me while I was in hospital, demanding that I discharge myself and come get my children.

How could I do that, when I couldn't even walk? He would abuse me for being sick and in hospital, and constantly play his nasty games. If it suited him I would be able to talk to my children. I wanted it all to end. Seeing so many women come and go, my emotions everywhere, something had happened and I felt no hope at all.

CHAPTER 11

My Darkest Hour

My time in hospital, I had regular visits from a Social Worker and she could see I was deteriorating in all ways. So the day that the doctors walked in and stood in front of me and told me it was too dangerous to continue with the pregnancy and that they had a c- section booked for me. I was so relieved yet scared because the doctors had warned us, due to all the high doses of methadone and morphine I had been given, Perinatal Addiction had occurred and they expected her, to be bright red and constantly screaming. But that wasn't the case; she came into this world perfect.

But she had to be placed in the neo natal unit because she was born so early. With only needing a small amount of oxygen, and a tube to feed her, other than that she was a true miracle. I had had staples from the C-section, but that did not bother me at all. I was able to walk around, because in those seven weeks, there were a lot of times where I thought I wasn't going to make it and I would not get to meet my beautiful daughter Miranda.

The day came, that the doctors said that she was right to come home, that they would fly us back to the local hospital; I just wanted to go home. living at pete's it was not the best place for my baby girl to go back to. Like Eric, Pete would get into intoxicated states. I could see he was not happy in his life either. I was able to read him so easily, knowing how lonely he was. Constantly telling Eric his brother was not well inside. I didn't know why or how I was able to do this. Maybe it was because I was the same? We would both put a mental cover over it and laugh things off.

But I knew, I tried to look after Pete as much as I could, always a soft spot for him. No one else saw his loneliness or even tried to understand him. Maybe I was meant to see through him and see his real side? I found myself always telling him, he had so much going for him. I asked Eric to invite him out with us, without knowing I was digging the hole deeper and deeper. That was because I began to feel suffocated. Always Pete and Eric, it was like I was in a three way relationship. It was even harder when Suzy, Pete and Eric were together.

I felt like I was being pulled in three different directions, not ever wanting to upset any of them, but deep down I was jealous of the love and relationship they all had. It wasn't the healthiest thing I could do, but I couldn't help it. Eric's Mum, was a very unique individual. Nothing like I anyone I had ever met, so blunt in a funny way. I really didn't get close to her though, why would I when Eric wasn't? I hadn't like Sharon at all when I had started seeing Blake, but Mary was different, one of a kind.

Erics's dad, was different in his own ways as well, so easy for me to read. He did not approve of me and I was barely tolerated. For years I would tell Eric how lucky he was to have his family, and not to be so cold towards any of them. So when Miranda came along, I was not sure what to expect.

The family had taken my children and I in, it didn't matter, how much they tried to make me feel or believe that they were my family, that I wasn't missing anything, but it never worked. It wasn't like I didn't try, but not belonging anywhere in my life, this wasn't any different. Constant thoughts going through my head, that no one loved me, and no one ever could. I had never seen Eric love someone so much, he absolutely adored our daughter. I would sit watching him, knowing that the love he had for her, I had never had for any of my children.

If what I saw in his eyes for Miranda, was love, then it was confirmed, I never once had, had it myself. It was this absolute realization that put me on a path of no return. What was wrong with me my emotions were everywhere? But it wasn't emotions; it was just one, anger! I didn't know why, usually I was really good at hiding it from everyone. And once again,

I started pushing Eric away. I knew I did love him, but fear wouldn't allow me to give anyone my heart, not even to my children. Just like so many times in my unfulfilled life, I was losing sense of everything.

But this time, my great adaptability, had disappeared. Not even the auto pilot button worked, I missed my children and if Eric's family could rejoice in our daughter's birth then I wanted my family too. I wanted them to know that my life had changed so much. After years of not seeing them, I was put in contact with my Dad and my older brother Shane. After talking on the phone for a week, it was agreed that we would travel down to stay with Suzy and John, before travelling interstate, to see my dad and brother.

My children had finally come home after not seeing them for months, and only being able to talk on the phone with them, if Blake allowed. Before we left, I had seen the baby nurse about the gunk that was forming in Mrianda's eyes and nose. She was six weeks old; I was advised just to give it a saline cleaning, which was a relief, because I refused to go back to the local hospital. Their duty of care was not adhered to, I was horrified when I had to be flown back to there, when I left the neo natal ward with her.

I had just started her, drinking her bottle at two weeks because prior she was tube fed. That night, I left her there, in their care. After two months from being home, I just wanted to shower and sleep for weeks, first thing in the morning returning to the hospital they had tubed her again because it was easier then feeding her her bottle. Pete's house was definitely not what you would call homely. But it was where we were living at the time. The exciting day came when we left to go meet my dad and brother. It was amazing; he was so warm and gentle. Something I had not seen before, he loved his grandchildren they all did.

I'd come up for my brother's birthday party to give him a gift, for that day I had forgotten myself and all of my issues, and thoroughly enjoyed watching my children being loved and adored. Call it fate, but my older brother Wayne had shown up at their house that weekend. He had never met our father. I'd find out months later, that they all became very close.

had been worried about Miranda all weekend, she was refusing her bottle. After a long drive back, when we got to Suzy's, I opened the car to take her out. He skin had started to turn blue. It was too late to call for an ambulance, so Eric drove me and Miranda to the nearest hospital, I was hysterical. I got her out of her car seat, leaving Eric in the car out the front and ran as fast as I possibly could into emergency. I was gently shaking, rocking her and I felt her body go limp in my arms.

There was a man in front of me, complaining about a broken toe, there I was standing having to wait for the nurse, who must have seen me because she looked past the guy with the broken toe, and asked me if everything was ok? I managed to cry that there was something wrong. She pushed a button, hurried me into a room, grabbed Miranda out of my arms and gently plopped her onto a bed, to resuscitate her. People were coming from everywhere! I couldn't understand and I instantly blamed myself, but not only did I Eric did as well. I had been sick for weeks coughing; maybe I had given her something.

I just needed someone to tell me everything was okay, I needed someone to hold me and tell me it was just a bad dream and tell me to wake up, but that didn't happen. Because it wasn't okay, nothing was okay. We got ushered out when told they had intubated her. I couldn't understand what was going on, and Eric was beyond angry. In between all of this going on, Suzy had driven up to the hospital with my children. I did not want to be outside in the parking lot, I wanted to be inside with my daughter. My head was spinning so fast, my heart beating like it was going to leap out of my chest.

I was going to lose my baby girl, Eric not wanting to hold me nor even be next to me. The doctors explained to us, Miranda had to be airlifted to the big hospital to be put into intensive care. I couldn't cope, it wasn't there arms she had died in, and it was mine. It wasn't them that went through the pain that I did. I needed Eric to understand I wasn't coping, but he refused, as I was out in the parking lot making sure my children were okay, he walked out and told me I had to go on the plane. I informed him I was already ruled out because of how sick I was. I couldn't comprehend why he was so angry! What right did he have to be angry? We were supposed to support each other. And how could I be the blame? I would never do anything intentional to hurt MY children.

She'd been fine except for the gunk I had been clearing from her eyes and noise all weekend following what the midwife had advised me to do. I couldn't describe the feeling that was inside of me. I couldn't do this, I just couldn't be here, what other horrible joke or event could happen in my life, and how much was I meant to suffer? Eric wouldn't even let me near My baby girl, and he left to go on the plane. I tried to conceal the emotions and erratic thoughts, but I could not. The fury and sorrow, burning up inside of me. My partner was supposed to be with me. And not cold.

Before she got airlifted back the doctors told us to prepare ourselves, because they did not think she was going to make it. I couldn't think straight, all I knew was I had go back to Suzy's, pack my children up and prepare to make the long drive. Suzy came with me and drove, honestly I thought it was better with me not there. But what I felt was different. I was consumed with fear, gut wrenching, gripping, terrifying fear. I did not want to be here. I couldn't feel.

In the weeks leading up to this, something horribly wrong was happening in my soul. I couldn't seem to do anything right, and when I got down there, things turned from bad to worse. It was like Eric had not even wanted me to be there. I just wanted to be with my daughter, I needed someone, anyone to tell me she was going to be okay, but instead Eric screamed at me, with such hate and left me in shock. The frostier he became, the more fury was building inside of me. The only defence I ever had was I could hurt people with my words. So that's what I did.

I spent a night in a hotel, because the day I got down there, Suzy too blamed me and screamed at me, what was wrong with these people? How could I have done this? I didn't want to be present, I couldn't feel or comprehend what was going on? I wasn't even able to go to the hospital to even be with her, as no one could watch my children. Not one word of support was spoken to me, not one caring word at all, not even when I rang my own father for morale support. His reply was, what did I want from him? What the hell did he mean? I needed my dad to tell me that it was ok that everything was ok.

I needed someone to make me believe that they cared, but no one did. That night I didn't mean to but I started to take it out on my other children, I wanted to be with my daughter, and part of me blamed them that I couldn't be with her. They had witnessed the huge fight that Eric and I had out the front of the hotel and they witnessed me call him again and again just to hang the phone up in my ear. What had I done to deserve this? The darkest moment in my life and I had no one, My beautiful children were with me, all I wanted to do was be away from them. I should never had, had any children. They didn't ease my pain or deep loneliness, no one cared.

Or even liked me, because if they did I would not have been in the motel room by myself, trying to put pieces together that would not stick. The next morning I was able to go up to the hospital, Eric was less hostile, but I didn't care as the damage was done. As I walked in, my baby girl was awake. She had fought for her life. I was so thankful. I held her so tight! I knew it was Eric's love that had saved her he was the one who sat with her all night because I was too busy fighting the demons.

I needed to know, what was wrong and what had happened. I was informed by the doctors that she had, had golden staf, the gunk that the midwife had told me to use saline water on, was actually golden staf. Thankfully our baby girl thrived, and within days she was able to come home. Unfortunately I couldn't face it. I could only take so much. My strength was disappearing. I knew I wasn't as strong internally as I used to be. The first thing I did when I got home was send my children to their Grandparents, I needed a break. I needed a break from my life. To me I was stuck in a glass jar looking outside at everything. Who could I tell? They would all think I was crazy. I thought moving away, would help cure me.

Eventually Eric got a job, and was elgible through his job agency to receive accommodation and stay down there till we could arrange something. For a few days the lovely little cabin we called home was great. While Eric was working I spent my days admiring my little survivor. Mesmerised by her strength, yet still living in a daze, no family or friend to speak off, missing my children but knowing it was better for them being where they were because without a doubt they were getting all the love they would ever need.

One of the nights that Eric got home, he had found out that old friends were staying in a cabin two minutes away. He went to catch up, The whole time he was gone, my head clouded, what was he doing? Never once did he stand up for me and then I began reliving what had happened just recently, it was literally just over a week earlier that my daughter had died in my arms. If anyone had asked me what I was feeling I would not have been able to describe it, there was no name for it.

Eventually Eric stumbled in the door, there seemed something different about him, such a scary look in his eyes like nothing I had ever seen before. Something wasn't right, something erupted inside of me, I told him I was leaving and that I couldn't cope. I couldn't tell him how I was really feeling, that I didn't want to leave him, I had wanted to leave this life. Before I had a chance to sit down and calm my erratic behaviour, to my astonished shock, and heart break, Eric punched me. He kicked me, pulled my hair slammed me into the walls, into the small bathroom. And just like many years ago, my head was smashed once again into a basin. I couldn't get away; he was so big and strong, hitting me again and again, and he then threw me out of the door. I knew this wasn't Eric, what was wrong with him he would never hit me.

I stumbled to the payphone and rung my Brother's, but I didn't ask for the police to be called, I knew he didn't mean it. And even more so, I shouldn't have let my anger, and my nasty words, come out. My brothers wanted to call the police but I begged them not too. I told them I was fine, and hung up the phone. I was in so much shock, I sat outside the cabin as I cried and smoked cigarette after cigarette knowing Eric was asleep in bed by now.

I wanted to check in on Miranda, and make sure my baby girl was okay. I needed to go to sleep, as I lay on the bed, I saw the torchlight. And I heard the knock on the door. I knew it was the police. I thought if I told them it was a mistake they would leave us alone. But they had seen my injuries and literally threatened to call the department of child safety if I did not go with them because of Miranda being involved. They made me do a statement and informed me nothing would come of it. Maybe just and AVO.

I tried to explain to them that it was completely out of character for Eric to even think about hitting me. But they had great delight and earlier that morning, they came back to the cabin, woke him up and took him away, because what I was made to tell them was enough for assault charges. I was too tired from the night before, so I went to sleep. When I awoke I thought Eric would have been back, It was when I rung the officer, I was informed that Eric had been taken to the watch house and that he had been taken to the court house. It didn't make sense to me as I had not asked for any charges to be made.

When I got myself and Mrianda to the courthouse, I saw eric there but he walked in the other direction. I caught up to him and asked him what had happened and he explained to me he was not allowed to talk to me or explain what had happened. What did he mean he wasn't allowed to talk to me? It wouldn't be hours later until I found out that the judge had said, he was had no contact with me until the next court hearing which was scheduled for two months later. My life was a wreck, how did all this happen?

Even when I rung my brothers to try and talk to them, I got rejected, I had nowhere to go again. I had two days left at the cabin and no idea what I was going to do. I knew one person that would help me, though I had left things unfinished with her, and that was Katie. I had been talking on and off with her. When I rung, I could hardly speak. All I did was ask if I could come up and stay with her. She had said yes I was more than welcome and to get up there. It just happened she lived ten hours away. So I arranged with Kevin and Sharon to meet me at their nearest train station so I could pick my children up so we could go.

I hated being back in the state, my heart was not there. I knew Eric couldn't text me back, but I sent him so many messages that I was sorry, that I loved him, trying to explain to him that it wasn't my fault. I made the best I could at Katies's because all anyone did there was sit in the garage drinking and smoking. Always people there I had no intentions of staying. There were good times. She had changed a bit, I had to try to put it all behind me and live the best way I knew how.

yet again I made the decision I could not put my children through it one more time, so when Kevin answered the phone I blurted everything out to him, and asked if they would come and get the children. They had not asked to be bought into this world or be bought into my horrible existence but over and over again I dragged them down my dark road.

Many hours, Katie would spend trying to talk me into moving up there and getting a place next to hers'. But this wasn't my home, I hated it, my heart was somewhere else, I would analyse Katies's life determined not to be stuck there. Over those two months Miranda and I spent so much time in the car, driving back and forth between the two states, I was determined in getting better, but that meant having my family back, I didn't want to sit around and drink. I was over that, the desire and determination to get back was so strong. Any low moments, I would smoke weed just to take the edge off. I put many applications in for houses and kept getting declined.

I started to think I was never going to get back there, but that couldn't be, I had to get my own home and set up our place ready for my family to come back. It helped having no radio in my car, because it gave me plenty of time to think. When I was at Katie's I could only stay for short periods of time. There were good times, but most of that, my heart and mind where somewhere else. The day I had completely given up, I got a phone call, saying I was approved for a beautiful three bedroom home on the river where I had desired to be. I was so elated, and relieved, with the help of friends and a complete stranger I finally had moved into my home after a thirty hour trip.

I was finally home, I had done it, I had accomplished it! it was the week before I had to go back to court and face what was going to happen. I didn't even know if Eric still loved me. The time for me to find out, arrived before I knew it. I could feel the anxiety walking up to the courthouse with Miranda in her pram. When I saw eric and his father, he looked so handsome, I knew if anything whatever the outcome I had to make it right for out baby girl. She'd missed out on her dad for long enough.

When I went in and saw the solicitor I told him everything, I had never asked to have assault charges pressed, I told him about Miranda being in hospital, he asked me what I wanted out of it. I simply told him I wanted to be able to make contact. When we went into the courtroom, I so hoped something wonderful would come out of it. To my absolute relief the judge was very understanding and though I was not the one standing being spoken to, he spoke to me and asked me questions. I walked away being able to contact Eric, and not too long after, he told me, he hadn't been able to stop thinking about us. All of those hours spent driving were worth it. I had my family back.

CHAPTER 12

The Nothingness

Eric was the first to come home, and a week later, Cameron and Amber, Jake didn't come, because of his Asperger's he was in a routine up with his grandparents and honestly I could not begrudge him of that. After the life my son had lived with me, we were finally getting our lives together. Eric had a good job, Cameron and Amber went to school, and I stayed at home with Miranda. It wasn't all roses, there were occasions where I would let the darkness take over and drive Eric to a place of anger. When we fought I always found myself telling him to get out. I couldn't help it; I knew I didn't mean it.

It Must have been one of my screwed up coping mechanisms, there were more positives than negatives, until for the first time in nine years, I let my family back into my life. It started with my older Brother wayne, we had been through a lot in our lives but I loved him. He came down for a visit and it was perfect, he had seen that Eric wasn't what he thought he was, he saw that I was happy. Wayne was not talking to our mother and had a falling out with our father, so I am really not sure how within weeks, my little sister Stephanie was visiting us, she was about to become an adult.

I invited friends that I had met through Katie down for a weekend, a father and son, to have a few drinks and BBQ because our Miranda was turning one. Time flew so fast, within a week, my life was turned upside down inside out, and left dangling. What was my reality as I knew it, was no longer. For a whole week, my mentally unstable sister would scream my house down, storm out the front door. I could not really understand what was going on. Luckily I had Wayne there with me, because I did not know who this girl was. The real-estate was really good to us, never once did we get a complaint, fall behind in our rent, and the agent loved coming for an inspection.

But in one night, we were given our marching orders, on that night I honestly thought Stephanie was going to die of alcohol poisoning, she scared my children, tried to sleep with my forty year old friend and even flirted with Eric. She was out of control and it was this reason, that I ended up talking to my step dad on the phone and through that, my mom via Facebook. Everything was going so fast that I didn't even stop to think what I was doing. My family wanted me back, and that's all that mattered to me. I had arranged to meet my step dad at McDonalds.

The bridges had been mended between Suzy and I and we had put our differences behind us, and they too were now living in the same state as well. It made life so much easier, when we would either pick Jake up or take Cameron and Amber for their visit. we would also get to spend time with all of them. My children didn't talk about their dad too much, and they began to tell me that they didn't want to be there if he was. No one knew the pain I suffered and it began to grow to phenomenal levels.

And after nine years, of not having a relationship with any of them except Wayne, we were packed up and I was living with them. After my initial reunion, I wanted to be close. It looked like they had changed so much. Stephanie had, had us kicked out of our home, Eric was not happy at all. No way was he going to come with us. He stayed with his mate for, four weeks while he was still working. I was starting to reconnect with my family again. They treated me so amazingly, and I even noticed they were helping me with my extremely unruly children; it gave me the courage to get Jake back home.

I was closer to my mum than what I had ever been in my whole entire life, they looked after me, and I began to really get to know my other sister Sarah. When I was younger she was the one I spent more time with, I tried to get close, but she was just too much like her father. Being an adult now, conversations came up with my mum. That before then I wouldn't have been able to handle, but I began to noticed that they were treating me like the eighteen year old that had walked out of their lives, many years ago

I missed Eric so much, I missed our home and what I used to know and I resented Stephanie for taking my life away. what I thought was help, I realised, was actually control. The subtle little comments they made about Eric, and they needed to know everything that I had been doing for the nine years and Before too long, there was conflict. The day my mother opened her mouth, and told me she had been warned about uncle Frank but still let him live with us in and take my life away, they lost me.

I was a victim, a scared little girl, my life descended faster than ever before, but I still needed them, I could not lose them again. I thought getting a home close by would be the answer. My mum and I had so many deep conversations, and then just as I remembered as a child, it was like nothing ever happened. I couldn't keep up, not when Eric didn't want to be near them nor talk to me, not when we would have fight after fight, or even that my children, were reliving, the controlled harsh parenting that I had.

I couldn't go on, all the old emotions turning into a cloud of black fury, just waiting to have the chance to erupt. The day it did, my step father had just threatened to cut my daughter's fingers off just as he had done to me when I was at the same age. I screamed at him, with pure hatred, how dare he? They were my children, they had no right. I tried to find good memories because I couldn't understand why I was there. All my memories were locked in a vault, with words of warning, NEVER OPEN. For years I couldn't work out why I could not remember, but my question was finally answered the day I found the video tapes of my childhood. I wanted to sit down with Sarah to watch them, and remember the good times.

Mum didn't want me to watch them though, but when she went out, Sarah put them on, I wish that she hadn't, out of four video tapes there was not one happy time. There may have been for Sarah as she was loved and praised, adored while the whole time my brothers and I were belittled and tormented time after time, tape after tape. That was it, it was all confirmed for me, right at that moment, not once in my life, had I ever been loved. I didn't have memories, because there was not a single good one.

The fury, inside of me, and the hate I felt towards my step dad returned, I couldn't stand being near him anymore, after stating he was a little harsh on us and being told, that I was still playing the victim. Not even when I had moved into my own home did they stop trying to control everything even my own children! I was told I was too soft on my children, that I was a soft touch and they took the reins. They had the strings, and I was the puppet, I thought letting my Brother Wayne move in downstairs would protect me. But that was the worse decision I could make.

My stepfather the monster and my mum the heartless control freak, always at my home, so it wasn't my surprise that I started to smoke more weed, drink more alcohol, and pop antidepressants like they were lollies, if I was high, then I was safe because I could not feel my emotions and the suffering consuming me. I just could not face reality as I was stuck, I didn't really know these people, they weren't really my family, and within four months of being in their presence they destroyed me. My partner had, been in a horrific accident and was lucky to be alive.

I blamed myself for that night, I begged him not to leave me up there alone with the strangers who controlled every part of my life. But he couldn't stand being near them, we had just, had a very big fight outside the front of their house, he drove ten hours and had a head on collision with a truck. Wayne had his downfalls, but for a while it seemed like he cared and they didn't. What was wrong with these people? Did they want me to be completely alone? Because of Eric's accident he could not work. He had no car, all that was left, was him coming up to live with us. I felt much safer in his arms, after my brother trying to get me to sleep with the first man, who I crushed on, Tristan.

I was just looking for friendship, and I knew he could get me ecstasy, butter would not melt in his mouth, even when he came around, flirted and tried to tell me to leave Eric, I was drawn to him for his intellect, the man could sell snow to Eskimoes, but I loved Eric! Because of all the hectic chaos and being completely out of control, I had not realized that I was pregnant, Eric was so happy, and I tried to be. It was a shock it took me time to come to terms with it all. Eric would rub my belly, and for a time, I was happy. I wanted the baby, until my mum and stepdad found out, and one night my stepdad came around, sat at my table, and talked to me about getting an abortion. He made me believe that I couldn't have another one, that basically I wasn't a good enough mother and that it would wreck my life.

He made me admit, that I had Jake because I needed someone to love and love me back, who was I kidding he was right. I couldn't hide it anymore, he was right, I didn't want another baby, just another life for me to screw up, and another child I couldn't love. The more they spoke to me about it, the more I believed it. I thought I had made my decision but my head was telling me something different to my heart and before I knew it my mother had made me an appointment on the day after my twenty seventh birthday.

I was supposed to celebrate my birthday the day before, it was the first birthday I had in nine years that I had my family, because every birthday since my eighteenth I would sit somewhere quietly and cry. It was the first cake since my sixteenth birthday. I know they were trying to make it a good day for me, but how could it be? I could feel this life inside of me, and the next day I was going to do the unthinkable. Eric refused to be with me nor have any part of it. I tried to talk to him to make him understand, that I couldn't bring another life in, I was torn after I realised I could have lost him, the man I loved.

How could I murder because that's what it was. How could I do that to our child? It wasn't easy, but what might confuse others, was the feeling that was inside of me. I couldn't even name it, it was like something I had never experienced, in all of the time I had been on this Earth. It came so fast and the next morning I found myself at the clinic. There was a man outside with a sign from GOD, it angered me. If there was a GOD he would have saved me a long, long time ago.

Walking up the steps, I needed Eric to be there, I needed him to tell me it was going to be okay and to stop me. My mum had offered to pay for it, so after doing that I sat down, they didn't say a word to me, they just sat there laughing about things. I watched all of the other girls come and go until it was my name called. I was taken into a little room and told to put on a gown and wait. What happened next was torture; they did an ultrasound and showed me the life inside of me. She had said I was ten weeks gone, the shock of how far I was and seeing that life inside of me, was too much. I shut down.

I was led into a room and put on a bench type bed, screaming inside, please I don't want to do this, but just like so many times before in my life, no words came out. I was frozen, even when I was given the needle I was screaming stop, but it was too late.

I awoke dazed and not feeling well. What had I just done? How could I live with myself now, after wanting to be dead all of my life, I had murdered an innocent life. I walked out without a word; we were apparently supposed to be stopping for lunch. They acted as if nothing had just taken place! I couldn't eat and felt so sick, I didn't care, what they thought was the way to cope.

I couldn't be near them; there was no support, no reassurance, nothing. I had to get away; I made my way back to the car, after throwing up. I wanted to sleep, just sleep and not wake up. I was empty there was nothing left, it did not take them long at all to turn against me, to ridicule me, having them stand in my front yard screaming horrible things, all because I refused to let them control me. I wanted to kill them I really did, what did they expect from me, to put salt on my deep wound, I was forced to pay back the money for the abortion, and as soon as I did, I was told, that my mum had, had an abortion that she regretted.

What was I hearing? What did this woman want from me? Did she want me to live her life? Is that what she wanted from me? To completely rip my heart out and leave me dead on the floor because that's what I felt. They never wanted me, not once did they ever love me, I needed to get away. Eric and I had started drifting away from each other because I wouldn't let anyone near me, I was a shell with nothing inside. Four months of having what I ached for and thought that was what was missing, I was in complete consuming darkness. There was no light at all, thankfully Eric got a job interstate, as soon as they knew I was leaving I was rejected and thrown away.

I begged Eric to get us a home, I didn't care if it was in a town, that had nothing he had a job and we were together, I was far from mentally stable, I needed to be constantly high or drunk every night to help me sleep. I couldn't be there for my children any longer, because I couldn't look after myself. I found it hard to get out of bed. A couple of months we lived there until I couldn't stand it, I started hitting into Eric. Something I had never done before. I don't think Eric knew what I was going through because it was never spoken about.

We were quite close to Suzy and John, Eric applied for a job, up near them to get us away from that place and he got it. He was supposed to go up and stay with Suzy but it was too much for me, he couldn't leave me there! I broke down in front of him and begged him not to leave me there. I knew that my boys needed a father figure and their pop was the perfect man for the job. It was agreed that boys would leave and live with the Grandparents until we got ourselves sorted. Blake's still constant belittling and verbal abuse when I asked for help wasn't a surprise, and at that stage I couldn't care what any of them thought of me. It didn't matter because it couldn't be worse than what I thought about and better still felt about myself.

No one knew, the silent tears I cried when I was alone, I felt that everyone had abandoned me, nothing I tried worked I couldn't come back from this. I couldn't pick myself back up, my unique ability to hide it was gone, and my adaptability was gone. When I moved up to Suzys I introduced myself to ice through an associate. I was a used puppet that had been thrown away. Completely destroyed, I tried to open up to Suzy one night, while I was high on the ice, to tell her I just couldn't live with myself anymore. I couldn't live, I was dead, there was nothing, all the years of trying not to feel, and now I couldn't feel a single thing.

But I just couldn't, I couldn't tell anyone and that's just how it had to be. Somewhere in my erratic scattered thoughts, I thought consuming my whole box of antidepressants would make it go away. But nothing, I knew what I was doing, I had known all my life that I was worthless, I was on the gas, ice and popping pills whatever I could get my hands on at the time, I decided that this was it and made a promise to myself, that I had the absolute strength left inside of me to do it. To surrender and take my own life.

My children deserved better and Eric certainly didn't need me around, all I ever did to anyone was to cause heartache and pain. Cause them to abandon me, abuse me, use me and throw me away. Because if I didn't I would be a loving person that wasn't trapped in a deep dark place, unable to see anything but the pleasurable thought of death. Thinking of the peace my family would have, I thought of telling Eric that I did not want my children to grow up not knowing each other. Everyone around me thought I was okay because I was high all the time, I wouldn't ever be able to talk about what was going on. I knew that the night I was going to do it, my boys would have to be there. I couldn't go this time without telling them I loved them.

As each day went by, the feeling of nothingness grew. A feeling of absolute emptiness as too did my desire to end everything. I didn't care about anything; no one could help me, for so long I had been beyond hope. I knew that apart from a few beautiful moments in my life I was pathetic excuse. I couldn't be a mother; I couldn't be a friend, a daughter, a lover, or anything. What use was my existence, everyone in my life was better off without me. It wasn't long before the perfect day had arrived.

My boys were down for the weekend, we spent a good day together as best as we possibly could. I made the decision that I was not going to be high that day, because that was how I was going to go. I had already purchased the drugs and made sure I had enough that would take me. Not my children's hugs so tight could save me; I was a zombie, a shell, a body with nothing inside of it. I didn't even know who I was. I had completely lost all sense of what reality was. That night, I spent time in the room with my children; I told them to please remember that I love you so much.

I watched them go to sleep, and when they did, I sat there, and I apologised for everything. I apologised to them for me not being able to be there for them, I apologised for every birthday I would miss, every moment that was their amazing lives that I would be looking down upon them, I spoke to my Amber about her first boyfriend and everything that I could tell her about what I wanted for her as she grew into a young lady, I spoke to my boys and told them to be strong for their sisters I asked them to make sure that Eric was loved and to tell their baby sister that I loved her and I wasn't alway's a dark person. I spoke to my boys about growing into strong, beautiful young men and to make sure that no-one was ever sad with my passing Everything that I could possibly say to them I told them while they slept, I knew I was saying goodbye. If I loved anyone it was my children but nothing I was heartless, I could not experience this sensation anymore. No one, could ever comprehend what had consumed me, and it was only a matter of time, for me, I had been treading the water of life, for far too long. And now, I was drowning; there was no point fighting for gasps of breath, because I didn't want to take one. I wanted to slip under the water and die peacefully, for all my organs to slowly shutdown as I was laying and looking up the stars.

After I left my children's room that night, I slowly walked down the hallway, I sat on Suzy's lounge in the lounge room, I took one last look at her and Eric mucking around in the kitchen, the drugs in my clenched hand. But something inside of me told me to look down, a sudden urge to look down took over me. Right there in front of me was a book, then I heard a voice say it's your destiny. I picked up the book, after being on so many drugs and losing all sense of everything I had to make sure, it wasn't a figment of my imagination.

It seemed like the book was glowing in my hand, the name on the cover, THE SECRET.

CHAPTER 13

Awakened

I sat there with the book in my hand, dazed, by the voice I had heard and by what I thought I had seen, and I found myself again, out of my body. But it was different I wasn't witnessing the cruelty of Humanity. I was witnessing what I did not realise at the time, My spiritual awakening. I read a little bit and then felt the urge to ask Suzy where the book had come from. The strange thing was, no one knew, they thought it was mine. As I started reading small little dots began to connect.

A lot started to make sense, a lot of what I had been doing wrong in my life. For me though, it was about my finances, and to bring us a happy home. Not for one second, was I aware of or did I even think that it would be the beginning of a great healing journey. I read the book over two days, and I wanted to teach Suzy and Eric everything that I was learning. My interest began in the universe. But unfortunately, it wasn't the end of my darkness.

Because of an unexpected incident and my cruel tongue I had completely alienated myself from Suzy and her little family. We had just moved into the wonderful big home I had wanted and we were doing fine the boys had come home and we were together again. Eric's job didn't last long, and Blake was seeing my children every second weekend. I had completely stopped smoking weed and barely drunk alcohol, so I couldn't understand why again, my life was descending.

I wasn't happy no matter what I did, we had good times but I noticed the same old feelings coming back up. The day after my birthday, Pete had, had a horrific car accident. Eric had to go down to be with him, he was in a very critical condition. Some how I knew Pete would come back, and told Eric to have faith and keep positive. Because for some reason, I knew Pete had his own journey.

For a while, I was able to control my still chaotic emotions and anger, before long it got the better of me and I became completely psychotic towards Eric. I couldn't help it and I didn't know where it was coming from, I created my first step along my journey, when I asked Eric to go and this time he did.

I regretted the words as soon as I had spoken them, but this time something was different, something told me to let him go. Then three days later, the strong feeling told me to follow him. How was I supposed to take my children and just follow him? The feeling did not go away so again, the boys went to live with their Grandparents. I couldn't do anything. I gave all my stuff except my bags and a few pieces away. I didn't know if I was thinking clearly, but there was a drive and a determination and I just felt like I had to follow it. I knew my boys were safe, but I didn't have a clue where the girls and I would end up nor what was in store for me.

I was scared but there was something happening, it felt like there was a war going on inside of me. We ended up in a caravan for two weeks, and after being in contact with Eric and talking things through I was able to apologise. His family did not approve of his decisions, but they also didn't know a lot of things that had happened between us, only what they wanted to but that was fine with me. I didn't know where to go from there. For a few weeks we ended up at an old acquaintance of ours. After realising that nothing had changed, we spent another four days in van in two different caravan parks.

One afternoon out of nowhere, Eric suggested to me we should move to an amazing place, we had visited one day and I had loved it, so green and luscious, I always found myself feeling better in nature, I made a few phone calls and just as I was about to give up after literally living in the car, we just spent a weekend with my boys, I made one last attempt to see if anyone would do share accommodation. For once we were lucky; our housemate was really lovely but as time passed as it normally would things turned sour. I desired and ached for our own place.

One morning as I was in town, I had a feeling to go to the library, and to go to the section, on metaphysics and spiritualty. I sat onto the chair and I looked at all the shelves, wondering what I was doing there. And then out of nowhere, two books jumped out at me. They literally fell off the shelf; it was these two books that completely opened my eyes and made me realise quite deeply, that I needed healing. The titles where, You Can Heal Your Life by Louise Hays And Ask and You Shall receive.

I was amazed, the more I read the more I craved, but it was these two books, that I read over and over again, until I awoke one morning, and had the thought, that I needed to see a healer. At this time, I didn't know what energy healing was. Three phone calls later, I was led to Kira. A beautiful light, funny, bubbly lady. I never had my tarot cards read, let alone be asked to hand someone a piece of jewellery that I had been wearing, I was very anxious and not knowing what to expect.

What came out of my first reading was the deepest crying that I had ever experienced in my life. She told me things about myself that I hadn't told a soul. She told me exactly how I was feeling. She knew my body had been raped over and over again. And she knew, that I spent my life feeling dead. Leaving that day, somehow I knew, that I had a long way to go, and it was not going to be easy, if things so deep were able to come up, then what else was there that needed to be released? And was I strong enough?

CHAPTER 14

Into the Light

I t was this time that I learnt about Angels and guides and the faith was instilled in me, to believe in GOD. For many long years I had believed there was no GOD. Now I knew different. But I perceived GOD different for some reason. Churches started annoying me, and I couldn't understand why? And I wouldn't for some time to come. I started to notice that because so much was changing inside of me, that I began to think Eric and I weren't meant to be together and more than ever I started pulling away, I don't know how he put up with me, and all darkness that was rooted deep in my being, but he did.

When I made the last final decision, that my boys were to come home and move into our own place. the truth was being revealed about how evil Blake really was when no one was around. They did not want to be there when he was around. I thought that after quite a few sessions, with Kira that I was healed. She had become not only my friend, but my children had adopted her as their Grandmother.

We were supposed to move into a big five bedroom home, but the landlord took all my money, and had me evicted. It lasted two weeks, my relationship with Eric had reached what I thought was the end almost to the boiling point. He moved into his own little caravan, to me it just seemed like he didn't care. my children helped me to pack store and clean the house. We were homeless and I had only enough money for a few days at the caravan park. Eric may have been cold towards me but was an amazing father.

I needed to rest and because he was only three minutes away he took Miranda for me. As heated as it would become between us, given time everything would settle down. There was a powerful attraction between Eric and I. Mine and my children's accommodation was up at the caravan park, I had no funds and absolutely nowhere to go. the Salvation Army, gave us four nights in a motel for the my children and I. I placed adds on the local websites trying to find a place for us, with one day left at the motel, I was becoming Frantic. Day's spent ringing around everywhere I possibly could; I literally had lost all hope. I begged and prayed for help.

When I was younger I found myself asking anyone even Satan, anything to get me out of the situation or take me away, but now I was praying to the angels, please for my children let us have a home, my prayers were answered. That night I got the phone call that saved us and changed my life completely. It was from a lovely man who had a house that university students were moving out of. He had seen my add on the website it was my prayers answered we moved in with nothing and gained everything. Andy was amazing, so generous, compassionate and thoughtful. He helped me with food, and I didn't have to pay a bond nor the first weeks rent.

After talking to him and getting to know him, he introduced me to the Sedona Method. And like I had found, I was drawn to it, almost addicted. Everything that was starting to open my mind and self, I would go over again and again. I was starting to feel there was no longer numbness through the Sedona Method and learnt that I lived in apothy and fear. I learnt how powerful it was to accept in the moment

The Sedona Method was only the beginning, but it was a powerful step, I knew I was still closed and there were parts with the method that I struggled with. No matter how hard I tried I could not forgive, especially myself. I started to notice, how strong my family was around me. because it was not an easy journey. Not at all.

Particularly, when I went from not being able to feel anything to all different emotions flooding me, I could laugh for a minute, cry and become completely outraged the next. I didn't know it was my whole lifetime, of repressed emotions and feelings, being finally released. Eric had started coming over on weekends and spending time with us, and eventually, we decided to give it another try. It was always a two steps forward and eight steps back process to me, I didn't realise, it was because subconsciously, if I started leaving myself vulnerable I would close back up, I still had trouble even considering opening my heart. I would never let anyone know how scared of life I really was. But for some reason I kept, trying I couldn't stop, on most days the fear would grip me. But it was what was happening inside of me. That could I not stop.

I thought I was confused soul, everything I wanted I feared, I hadn't begun to realise I had literally only scraped the surface, my next stepping stone happened to show up in email it was from a truly inspiring energy healer in America. Her name was Christie Marie Sheldon. For months, I had been using the same affirmation, unlimited abundance comes easily and effortless to me. It just so happened, that the program, was called Unlimited Abundance.

I had no idea what was about to be opened up for me.

It was at this time, that I started taking an interest in meditation, but it would leave me frustrated, time after time, I could not stop the thoughts enough to experience what everyone had been talking about.

CHAPTER 15

Return To Me

The Unlimited Abundance Program was the best thing that could have happened to me. I could literally feel the old energy blocks leaving. I started getting weird sensations all over my body, like it was vibrating, it was at this time, that something else showed up for me that I learnt about vibrations and what level people vibrated at. I was determined to live in high vibrations of love and joy. The night I finished the Unlimited Abundance Program for the third time, my body was vibrating all over, I felt the need to close my eyes. I closed my eyes folded my legs in my chair.

And I had an experience that not even words at the time could describe.

All of the vibrating sensations, that I received from the Unlimited Program, would not match, the moment and the first time, ever I was able to meditate. After being interested in meditation for some time, hearing what people were saying, and reading three to four books on it. Not once, did any of that information, prepare me for what greeted me. I was taken to an absolute amazing place where I was greeted by the Arch Angel Gabriel.

I had completely left my body, but I wasn't anywhere that I had been before. Just like the Angel so many years ago that had come to me, he too had a message. But his was much more powerful, as he spoke the words that I was a beacon of hope for others, I literally saw a beacon of white light from my chest, and explained to me quite strongly that it was MY time. And then, he was gone, and I was back in my body, in the chair which was in my lounge room. It was incredible

I rung Kira straight away, and told her everything, she did not doubt it, because only in our last session, she told me I was the light in the darkness and a bridge, more profound experiences were yet to come to me. I craved the guidance every day, and being in the presence of the angels. I felt I belonged with them more than I did in the physical realm. The more time I spent meditating, I began to realise my abilities. I started feeling a strange sensation between my eyes. I hadn't realised that my third eye had opened.

My ability to read people had grown into something far more, the most amazing day of my life was the day I felt real love. I was in meditation and I was struggling a lot more than usual on the earthly, I could feel my soul wanting something, because I knew we all were spiritual beings in a body, I cannot describe the feeling that I was experiencing for weeks. I knew it was big, something big. I just didn't know what. This day I found out, and this moment would stay with me for the rest of my life.

My words and description could, would and never will do justice, All I can do is try my best, I saw the, brightest golden light, you could ever imagine, I could still feel I was in my body, and tears running down my face. They were tears of pure joy, unconditional love, then just like a vortex I was transported, to the most amazing space that I ever experienced in my entire life, The word GOD, so strong in my mind and body, there was nothing but a feeling of, all I could describe as peace, bright colours and images that I really could not describe to you, colours that didn't have names. I then saw myself before I was birthed into this world. I saw what I was here for, I saw myself drinking out of a cup, and jump into an almost vortex looking lake and then birthed into the world.

Words so strong, remember what you are.

I was able to ask questions, I knew I was with GOD, it wasn't a man, it was the brightest light ever. I heard the words, your time is now. I was informed I could ask questions, I was shown, that I was a bridge, in which I saw thousands of people walking over into the light It was the most amazing experiences, not even words are justifying. I'm not sure how long I was in that space for.

I knew in all my heart and being that I was in the presence of GOD. It wasn't vibrations that I was feeling; it was like electric currents rushing through my body, sending tantalising sensations, through each cell. And that's how I felt when I opened my eyes. I noticed on the clock, that I had been gone for an hour and a half. And then I could feel my damp face, from the tears of joy, which were still pouring from my eyes.

After grounding myself, I had to go and tell Eric what had just happened, but like every human, he called me crazy and to stop living in my dream world, because if someone else had told me they had been in the presence of God. I too would have instantly doubted them, I learnt being with GOD, I had chosen everything, I had agreed and signed a contract for absolutely, everything. Nothing on it was a mistake, and not one thing, that was not meant to happen, happened. I chose my lessons and I even chose all of my perpetrators to come in, the Revelations that I had experienced were beyond profound. Not for one second did I doubt it.

Every day the guidance was my time is now, I could feel something big about to happen, but I still wasn't aware of what it was. Every time I was in the higher realms I did not want to return because to me it felt like I belonged there, with the angels and all of the light beings. It felt like my community. I shared everything with Eric, there was nothing I wanted to keep from him and tried to make him understand that I was changing, and things were starting to happen to me that even I couldn't understand.

Then all of a sudden my journey began to gain speed, I couldn't stop it. My guides and angels were still helping me with inner work, I was far from the place I was destined to be. Not only did they give me guidance, they would give me tools and gifts, gifts of anything I needed. Courage, endurance, integrity, I was given a sword of light to help me through the darkness and I was able to ask them for anything, anytime I felt I needed something I would ask. I would literally feel it in my body; I would feel the energy currents, rushing through my body into my hands.

And then I felt the gift I had been given.

At this time in my life, Tristan had made contact with me again; I had started to believe that my guidance was that he was a lover from a past life, so to me that meant we were to be together. Anything, to distract me from my unfulfilled relationship. I completely believed that Eric and I were over, but I did not know exactly how wrong I had perceived it. It was Tristan, which made me pick up my pen one day, to help him understand how far I had come. And if I could do it, he was more than capable of it. I wasn't in love with him, yes maybe I would flirt a little, but I began to become frustrated when all he would do, is ring me and tell me how horrible his life was. Not only being told by him, but I could sense it, I had become very aware of it because I was very intuitive.

So after a phone call from Tristan, I went upstairs, and out of nowhere I picked up a piece of paper and began to write, but honestly I didn't know where it was all coming from. As I was writing the emotions were flowing thick and fast, I felt the nothingness again, the need for death. If I had of been able to put the pen down, it would have ended it but I could not stop writing. When I was finished that night, I honestly did not know what I had just written, because of memories that I didn't think could resurface, that I would ever know came to me. Every time I wrote something, I would see the memory; feel the emotion as if I was there. I was watching it all.

But I couldn't just write I needed to read it to Triatan, the first words that I ever put on the page, so one night I wouldn't take no for an answer, and I read it to him over the phone. There was an eerie silence and then an angry cry. He was in shock, he was angry and then he cried. His words to me, why would you do that? How could you do that? That just flew straight through my barriers and hit me in the heart. He said no one had been able to do that, that it was how he was feeling. I just replied, because I have been there and explained that, I felt every moment of it, experienced every part of it.

That night when I went to sleep, I dreamt a powerful dream and I saw a book. Just like all my abilities I was able to get messages in my dreams, able to decipher, things that needed to be received. I became that amazing in my dreams that my higher self would narrate them.

When I awoke the next morning, I felt the need to meditate, but this was different, I knew my life was just about to change and the big thing that I could feel was just about to be answered. So when the Arch Angel Gabriel appeared and guided me that I was to write a book that would help heal and bring hope to many others. I was the beacon of hope; it started making sense to me. But it wasn't easy, I needed some confirmation of what was being asked of me, even though intuitive I still didn't believe in myself, so I went to see Kira.

On the drive to Kira's, I am not sure if it was intuitive, but I was taken back to a memory of one of my sessions with her, and she had said to me she couldn't wait to read my book, a light bulb went off then and there. Wow she had seen it; I was really meant to write a book. How was I meant to write a book? I had never written anything, I had never accomplished anything; it wasn't just that, a very powerful feeling overcame me. The fear, which I would have to face, everything.

The fear, that I couldn't remember my life, the memories were gone. But I had to have faith, because that's what I was guided. I didn't realise that as hard as it was to write every word, feel every emotion, that it was healing me. I was letting go, there were moment where I couldn't pick up my pen for weeks, I couldn't face what had to be released. At this point of time, we were moving out of Andy's. He and The house had served their purpose to me and it was time to move on.

I was starting to worry, but I had been guided for every day that week that our new home was turning up. And just like that, it did. I had also noticed that all my life, I was able to see some good in people, even though I walked where angels dare not tread, but now I could see so much more. I could feel so much more, and it was starting to become a problem in my relationship. I was literally transforming at a fast rate. It wasn't all about being positive, it was about seeing the good in everything, knowing the reason for everything. If it was not meant to be then it wasn't meant to be.

Accepting things that occurred, I was connected to higher self every day. So it wasn't just angels and guides, it was my own higher self. I couldn't live with Erics's negativity, and could see as well that he was living in fear. I started to notice, that he had taken on all of my stuff. Not as deep as what I was, but he was in his own darkness. I tried to help him, and constantly would think to myself, if I couldn't give my partner hope, if I couldn't help him see the good and bring him into the light, then how was I supposed to fulfil my purpose?

I couldn't have him in my life anymore, his darkness just too much for my light. I hadn't realised though, that my light was dimmed, I asked Eric to move out and get his own place, I thought living apart was what I wanted. Eric worked in the town over, so he found a little flat near his place of employment and I was okay with all of this. I loved him and I knew it, but I just couldn't be near him, It wasn't meant to be, because as much as what I had been thinking, I was guided different. That he would eventually join me in the light, that he loved me more than what I could see, that he cherished me, and it was the day that he was supposed to move into his place and us into ours, that something changed in both of us, we couldn't leave each other, and he told me for the first time that he wanted to stay.

I couldn't help but to cry, because I could not work out what was happening. The realisation that I couldn't live without him in my life and I had to be patient with him. After only living in our new home, for four weeks, I could feel something happening, it was my next big step. In one of my sessions with Kira, I was the one who was told to free my mother, that I had taken on my mother's darkness, that all my life wanting to be dead, living in the darkness, was actually my mothers. I was literally living her life, her beliefs and her thoughts.

I had taken on her contract and not my own, I had taken on her lessons. When Eric was at work one night, sitting on my lounge quietly, a vision came to me, I was writing a letter to my mother, I was letting her go, even forgiving her. This surprised me because the night before, in my dream, I had screamed at my mother. Something I had never done before, I knew I had to do it, I knew it would have meant something for me, something would have lifted for me, so I sat down with my pen and paper and wrote.

I had written everything I had repressed as such a young child, a lot of anger came out, I wrote how much I hated her, how much I was angry at her for not loving me, for never allowing me in my whole entire life, to feel love, to give love because then maybe I would have been a better person. Even though I had a better understanding as to why things happened in my life, it was my inner child that had to be released, I needed to get out everything I had felt in my life.

Eight pages later, I was able to forgive, I was able to forgive the one person out of all the monsters that hurt me the most, made me feel the most. Hours later, of literally mourning the loss, forgiving and letting go, I took it outside and I burnt it I watched as every page burnt into the dirt. Ashes to ashes dust to dust.

The next morning I was in meditation, when Arch Angel Michael, bought my mother's spirit to me. He was taking her away. She left me with one message, that she loved me and to live the life that she never could. I had just had a spiritual death to my mother, and after days of crying, I knew it was done. It was finished, my connection completely broken, my energetic cord completely cut. All I was able to feel was compassion towards her, one of the hardest things I had ever done, turned out to be, one of my biggest blocks, released.

I was learning more and more as each day went by, I was a student of life. I had been told I had to watch my third eye, because it was completely expanded and I was taking so much in, but I didn't mind because I loved it, every minute of it, I asked for a new realisation every day and without a doubt I received. At this time in my life, I was given, in its own way, the miracle of cutting all ties, with Blake and his family.

The circumstances took me to the darkness for two weeks. I was now in the light and I would never go back there. I had to be the light for my children, because I had only just realised, that Blake was my daughter's monster. I vowed and declared that I would never let her live the life, which I had. I would never allow her to walk my path, and like hell was she going to take on anything of mine. I had become aware quite strongly, watching the dynamics of my family, that not only, was I learning to love myself, I was teaching my children the same thing. It wasn't easy, far from it, especially with my daughter Amber.

Whenever they had wanted any form of affection in the past I was unable to give it. Something inside of me would make me become angry, agitated, but I knew it was the fear; the fear stopped me from everything. The fear of love, the fear of opening up to anyone, the fear that they would see my soul. So if I had ever thought, for one second, that I was healed, I was far from it. I had only just touched the surface really, I held so much inside of me that needed to be released and let go. I had so much shame and guilt, and blame, fearing to even give any part of myself, because one session in meditation, I had realised, that I feared humanity, I feared the Earthly Realm.

It was always two steps forward and eight steps back, every time I thought that was it, I could give myself, I could trust, and even maybe love.

It was like I would let go of something then something would come in its place. But there was never any time that I wanted to give up. I needed to keep going, I started this journey and I was not going to stop. I needed to be free, free from everything that had held me back, free from the fear that I lived in.

I started having visions of myself standing on a stage talking to people, teaching, showing that they too could heal. I thought for a while that I was just dreaming, but the visions became so strong and along with the visions, the desire to get there, hold people's hands and tell them there was hope, but I couldn't do that until I was ready. Every week something new would turn up for me, something new to open my mind, and begin releasing my heart from the box it was kept in.

After visiting Kira, one day she told me I should see her next door neighbour; I felt that it was right for me as well. So I made my appointment, just like the first day of seeing Kira I was very anxious. I had learnt about Chakra's and your energy centres. I knew that Tanya, was about to read mine. When I walked into the little room and met her, she was beautiful, the only words that I could describe, beautiful, graceful and understanding. On my mind that day was my relationship with Eric.

Always the same thing, every time we began to get closer I would push him back away, I found my answer that day. We had so many energetic cords connected to each other, and it was love but my heart was closed. I was tied up in energetic binds of every bad and dark experience in my life. Did I want my heart to open? Yes more than anything. Did I want to feel love especially for my children and my partner? Yes. Did I want to trust humanity? Yes I did.

But I didn't know how, how was I supposed to open my heart when it had never been opened before? How was I supposed to trust when I didn't know what trust was? I left that day, got into my car and drove home. I walked into my house and I could not stop crying. I felt like I was a lost cause, I felt like I was so messed up that I couldn't return. What did I have to do? How much did I have to heal, to let go of? I did not only cry for one or two days, I cried for a whole two weeks. My children began to worry about me and Eric got very angry because he did not like seeing me that way.

At the time, I did not realise that at the time the crying, was me releasing everything, I asked for my guides and angels and GOD to help me release it all, help me open my heart. As well as what Tanya had told me that day she told me I had to keep writing, but not only that, that I had to read it to Eric. Even if he didn't want to hear it, his soul needed too. Because in a way, he was healing with me, I was healing, transforming and birthing back in to my authentic self. But still, my heart wouldn't open, and I asked my angels, guides and my higher self to give me the courage, to get through what I needed to.

I asked my beautiful partner to be patient with me because I was determined to give him my heart. I explained to my children that when I was crying I was healing and getting better for them.

Three times I had sessions with Tanya, it was the second last visit, as much as I didn't believe it she told me, that I was a blossoming flower with the old falling away. Along with the Abundance Program, I became a student at the Mind Valley Academy and purchased many of their programs. Every one of those programs more of the old fell away, more of the old I let go. I was starting to get confidence, the one thing I had always struggled with, was being able to speak. I would never speak from my heart, how could I when my heart was closed.

I wanted so much to speak my truth, but Tanya had told me my solar plexus, my power centre, was weak. I knew what I was sent here to be, but there was still fear. With all of this happening, I started to realise for the first time in their lives, that my children belonged home with me. I stopped wanting to send them anywhere, as much as the family dynamics were not the best, I loved having them home with me all the time. The hardest day of my life, the hardest step I had to take, I struggled with immensely. I was okay with forgiving others by now, but I was guided, I had to forgive myself.

For everything, all the blame I put on myself, for absolutely everything and when it came to forgiving myself, for putting my children through everything, and allowing them to live in the darkness with me, it was not easy at all. But that wasn't all; I had to forgive myself for not being able to love them. It's not easy to do, when I felt so much guilt and shame from it. When I was actually able to do that, I literally felt the relief in my body.

I was also going into my subconscious, and changing beliefs, thoughts structures and anything at all, that I had held true and was allowing to govern my existence. Every day I was working on myself, and I began to experience, fun, innocent fun. I started laughing for the sake of laughing, and I felt light, but yet I could still feel there was something I could not see, something that I had not become aware of. I asked for the guidance, and was advised to see Tanya, one last time, because with all the times seeing her, I knew myself what she was going to say to me.

But on that last visit, she asked me why was I there? And had told me, there was a reoccurring theme, in all of our visits, that all I needed to do was just believe absolutely, with every inch of my being, believe that I had actually come through it. That I was no longer that victim, that I no longer lived in the darkness. But that was hard for me to do, the fact that every time I released something and healed, something else would surface, all the emotions that my family would have to watch me go through. I was trying to work out how I was supposed to be doing that, how I could possibly do that, when I had never believed in anything before.

In that visit, she had told me I needed to let it all go, whether it was the bad the dark or even worse than that. That my way of releasing had been in writing. She told me that there was one more person that I had not forgiven and she could see my furiously writing everything that I needed to say to this person. On the drive home after leaving Tanya's who was she talking about? I had forgiven every one, all the men that had raped my body, all of the people that had done wrong by me, so I began to cry. Was this ever going to end?

I just wanted to feel peace and happiness, because she told me my heart was yet not opened. When I got home, I sat down and I asked myself, my higher self, who was it? Who was the person I had to forgive? almost instantly I intuitively received the monster in your book and I instantly knew, I hadn't really forgiven him and I asked my higher self again, apart from everything he put me through, what was it? What was the one thing, which needed to be done? And then again I was guided, that he gave me the belief all of my life, that I was worthless. And I saw memories upon memories, the words coming out of the monsters mouth, that I was worthless, I was never going to be anything, never amount to anything and that I deserved nothing. That was what it was.

All the times spent, changing my beliefs I had not even considered the core belief, the one belief that governed my life, I knew what I had to do. But before I could do that, I had to forgive. Tanya had been correct when she said, she saw me furiously writing. It was fury, not anger, not hate, fury. I had to forgive him now, for making me believe that I was worthless, I knew just like every other person I had to forgive, that it would set me free just that little bit more, so after I had forgiven him, and I had my cry and I let go, exactly just like my other forgiveness ceremonies, I burnt it into the dirt, Ashes to Ashes Dust to Dust. I loved the feeling, which would rush through my body, the moment the last ember had disappeared.

I was beginning to feel light, lighter than I ever had. Because the belief so strong in my core of my being, thirty days and thirty nights, for the first time in my life, I felt I was not worthless. And it was that night, which Eric was at work, my children in bed, that my lounge room filled up with the bright light. This time I was not in meditation, a light being, and angel appeared in my lounge room. But it wasn't just one, there were four or five, they basically told me, that I was to write my book, that it was my time, that I hadn't become aware how powerful I really was. That I was not yet healed, there was still more work to do. I didn't really need them to tell me this, because I felt it, every day it grew, stronger and stronger and my journey continued along with my writing.

There was a part of me, there was a very big part of me that could feel that when my story was finished that it would be the end. I was guided that I was a wounded healer, and every wounded healer by the time they came to their thirtieth birthday they would remember who they were. I was told by another very powerful, intuitive and energy healer, that I was an earth angel. I did not believe it of course, because I had been with the angels many times, I had died more than once, so earth angels did not sit right with me, I preferred healer, beacon of hope.

I become very aware, being a healer all of my life, that I would literally take others energies, to make them feel better. I was guided that I had done that all of my life and that I had started when I was in my mum's womb. I began to notice, that I was doing it all day every day. So it wasn't just my erratic emotions all my life, I had actually been living others, I spent all day cleaning my energy making sure I filled myself with light and love. It just wasn't working,

This was my next test; I had to start living in my own energy and not taking others. I noticed it was so easy, someone would walk into the room and I would feel anger, sadness, frustration and even anxious. All of the emotions, that no one likes feeling. I asked my guides, how could this stop happening? Because I preferred the light feeling, not the dense energy around me. My guides had said to me, that it was coming to me, my answer would be there within the week. My higher self-had told me that there was just three more stepping stones ahead of me.

I saw myself leaping over three stepping stones and ahead of me was this magnificent open crystal clear vision in front of me. I knew intuitively that it was to do with energy, because I had become aware of that energy was everything and it came in the form of an email, and it was from Coral Tuttle, an energy healer. It was called Chakra Seven. I loved it, every minute of it, and for weeks I worked on myself energetically, until I knew I was balanced.

If I thought I could feel vibrations and energy before, then I was under estimating myself. I could feel it in my hands and feet, I was told by a few people that I had advanced in such a short time, in my journey. What would normally take years, or even a lifetime, I had accomplished at great speed. I knew everything happened at the right time, even though I knew that I was capable of hacking my reality.

I hadn't thought about the two steps left, I was finally enjoying my life. The liberating moment, when I told myself I loved me was powerful, looking into my own eyes, and knowing, there was no shame attached to it. I began to say it to people, I began to speak my truth and spread my message of self-love and hope. I loved working with my mind and needed to understand more. I craved it, what some people would not even consider thinking I completely believed. Never once doubting or feeling it was too much, I couldn't even call myself a sponge because when you squeeze a sponge everything expels out.

I wasn't only full of knowledge I was full of wisdom, I found such a joy and inner passion, in teaching others what I knew. There were times, even with having the understanding, knowing, and being in the presence of GOD, I couldn't stand churches I couldn't stand religion. I wanted to pick the bible up and hit people over the head with it. Because to me they were living in closed beliefs, I couldn't understand why I felt the need to slap them in the face, with the truth of what I believed.

In guidance one day I had to ask this, as it wasn't in light and love, and my answer was, I was of much greater understanding and it all would be revealed to me soon. It took me a lot to be able to speak my truth, even if I felt it so strongly. I still had trouble expressing it. When I found my voice, my true voice, I started to talk to strangers about absolutely everything I had learnt. That we were the creators of our life and so much more. After telling myself and believing my entire existence, that I was stupid, that I didn't know anything, I now knew that I was actually intellectual. and aspired to talk on stage to people, whether it was tens, hundreds or thousands, anyone who needed hope or healing.

My soul knew who I was and what I was destined to be and not for one moment did I rest, always something else to heal and get through, I actually began to enjoy when something would come up and I could release it, let go and heal from it. I started this journey and I would continue until it was all gone. I was amazed at everything that was coming from my subconscious and just how much, pain, my heart actually held that needed to be released. I showed integrity always.

My abilities were amazing and I learnt that we were all capable of it, every single one of us, I was now able to receive messages in my dreams. I could simply ask my body and myself a question, and be answered. But I was still picking up and taking on others energies. During my days, I was always given signs from my guides and angels letting me know in their own way that I was on the right path. So the day came, that I found an angel card out of my pack on the floor.

As soon as I picked it up, I knew there it was my last step. I asked for Arch Angel Zadkeil, to help me release the last of my memories, to help me release everything that needed to be released because I had become aware, that subconsciously, there were two memories that I wold not let go of.

It was two hours later, after sensing, that he had been with me that I felt the need to meditate, and intuitively, I realised, that I was connecting to my three year old self. She was so scared, hiding in the dark. I picked her up, told her I was her and explained what had happened wasn't right, that I was here to release her, I told her I loved her and that it was unconditional, she was finally safe, and I was setting her free. She did not have to hold onto this story.

We were then both taken to my beautiful eternal garden, my sacred place and there waiting, were my guides and angels and the most beautiful playground that I had ever seen. I gave her one last hug and reassurance, I told her she was free to be happy and go and play. I turned and walked away and I was suddenly in the dark again. This time I knew so strongly, that I was with my ten year old self. She was lying on the floor curled up in a ball, so scared shaking, I knelt down, and so softly explained to her who I was and that she was safe.

I picked her up, and I tried to take her hand, but she pulled away and said to me, "No one loves me." I instantly grabbed her and gave her the biggest hug and said, I do, I love you, I care for you it's time for you to let go of all this, I'm you now, I'm happy. Yes it was wrong what happened to you, you deserved to be loved and not hurt. But it's now time for you to let go, I'm setting you free from this story and it's time for me to take you to a place of love. This time, hesitantly she took my hand as again we were in my eternal garden, but instead of a playground there were two swings. She looked up at me, and asked me to swing with her, I did as we held hands. I promised her she was safe with our guides and angels, that she was free to be happy, that all of the bad was now gone. I got off the swing, I gave her the biggest hug, I told her I loved her, but now I had to go and help other wounded girls and boys just like her. I walked away, as I did, I turned around one last time, I saw her so happy and smiling, her eyes were twinkling, then she waved to me.

All of a sudden I was then lifted up from where I was, I was surrounded by light beings again. I was told to turn around and look at my beautiful wings; I saw the most amazing wings, my wings. To my astonishment I was an angel, I had always been an angel, filled with such pure divine gratitude and love, knowing that all of my suffering, everything that I ever had lived through, was for the healing of humanity, it all made sense to me, every moment of my existence now made complete absolute sense to me. I am an angel, bringing the message of hope and love.

Lilly Faith

Arch Angel Gabriel, stood before me and spoke to me with the deepest love in his words. Welcome, home we have been waiting for you. I had one final last step to take.

Ashes To Ashes, Dust To Dust I was finally free.